THETFORD
A CENTURY
REMEMBERED
From 1900 to 2000
[Part Three]

David Osborne

Published
by
D. Osborne
2010

Published
by
David Osborne
107, Bury Road,
Thetford,
Norfolk IP24 3DQ
Tel: 01842 753379

British Library Cataloguing in
Publication Data
Osborne, David
Thetford - A Century Remembered
[Part Three]
ISBN – 0 9513484 4 2

Printed by Crowes Complete Print
www.crowes.co.uk

First Published 2010
© **D.J. Osborne, 2010**

Front cover: Red Lion Inn and the Market Place, c.1905.
Back cover: Red Lion Inn and the Market Place, 1951. [Photograph courtesy of Eileen Roberts]

ACKNOWLEDGEMENTS

As always there are many people that I must thank for helping me in so many different ways with the production of this third and final volume of *Thetford A Century Remembered.* For giving me original photographs or copies that are published in this volume I thank John Alvey, Derek Antrobus, John Ayton, Pat Boughen, Brian Boughton, 'Billy' Filby, Nora Goodley, John Grima of Baxter Healthcare, Hilda Kent-Woolsey, Neville Lockwood, Pat Pearson, Kathy Rae, Eileen Roberts, Cynthia Royle, Margaret Vidall and Stefan Zurowski.

For allowing to publish photographs from their collections I wish to thank Archant, Graeme Jacob of Studio Five, Thetford and Thetford Town Council.

My thanks are also extended to several people who have allowed me the use of photographs for this publication but, sadly, a lack of space has finally not permitted me to use them.

Once again my sincere thanks to Oliver Bone, Curator of the Ancient House, Museum of Thetford Life for allowing me access to the AHM's photographic archive. I also wish to thank Oliver for his valued and generous 'Foreword' to this publication.

A very big thank you, once again, to another good friend, exiled Thetfordian, Brian Carr, for his numerous general comments, diligence and patience while editing my original text. I also wish to thank two other good friends, Sarah & Stuart Wilson, for reading through and correcting the final draft of this *Thetford A Century Remembered.*

Finally, but not least of all, I thank my wife for her love and support.

ERRORS & CORRECTIONS
This volume allows me an opportunity to correct a small number of errors that appeared in the two previous volumes.

Thetford A Century Remembered
Page 14 delete: George Flack
Insert: George Flatt
Page 25 delete NOVABORD
Insert: NOVOBORD
Page 31 delete Jimmy Hume
Insert: Jimmy Hulme
Page 39 delete: and Guildhall Street
Page 44 delete: cylinderical
Insert: cylindrical
Page 58 delete: KING STREET 1984
Insert: KING STREET 1987
Thetford A Century Remembered [Part Two]
Page 10 delete: Ivy Benedykt [née Clarke]
Insert: Ivy Benedykt [née Sherwood]

FOREWORD
By
Oliver Bone, Curator,
Ancient House,
Museum of Thetford Life

Thetford has been fortunate in its historians. From the 18th century, Thomas Martin and Francis Blomefield gave us their versions of the town's story. Among others, the nineteenth century saw Hunt's work, and the twentieth century Alan Crosby's A History of Thetford. But for a visual feast combined with an accurate record and readable style we have the work of David Osborne. We are fortunate that the collective memory of the town has been so ably recorded for us by David. The Thetford a Century Remembered series is a great personal achievement and we congratulate David on his perseverance, eye for detail and scholarship. These books have put into the public domain a wonderful collection of evocative photographs reflecting many aspects of life in the town together with reliable commentary and description.

From my work as curator of the Ancient House, Museum of Thetford Life, I have known and admired David and his work for many years. His publications have been a valuable source of reference and enjoyment for many people, young and old alike. Whenever there is an enquiry at the museum that stumps us, we know where to turn. As an archivist and researcher David has tapped rich seams of information such as local newspapers and oral history as well as his pre-eminent collection of visual imagery of the town. He has always shown great helpfulness, good humour, generosity with his time and public spiritedness in all our association. His public talks and walks have always been great draws for Thetfordians who know the depth of David's knowledge in all things Thetford. But there is always something new to learn and David's thirst for knowledge about the town bears fruit in many ways.

Along with very many in the town I warmly welcome this new Thetford a Century Remembered.

Oliver Bone, Curator, Ancient House, Museum of Thetford Life

CONTENTS

INTRODUCTION

'Without these photographic images, would we have remembered Thetford's past so clearly?'

In 1996, it was my original intention to publish just one volume of *Thetford A Century Remembered*. However, aware of the fact that there were still many interesting and valuable images of the twentieth century yet to be published, particularly in a book or journal for general readership, it was followed four years later by *Thetford A Century Remembered [Part Two]*. Now, a decade further on, I am pleased to offer this third and final volume, providing yet more fascinating photographic evidence of twentieth century Thetford and its inhabitants.

As in the previous two volumes, various themes or subjects have been chosen, illustrating places, events and Thetfordians. Notwithstanding that each individual image provides a valuable record of life, once again I have added my own comments and descriptions alongside each photograph. I hope that this has given some extra value and meaning to the illustrations. Though I have repeated and touched upon some topics, individual buildings and parts of the town, I have endeavoured to provide fresh and additional information to that previously published. Once again, the photographs have been selected from a variety of sources and apart from a very small number of photographs, none of the other photographs included in this volume has been duplicated exactly in the two previous volumes of *Thetford A Century Remembered*. In total, over 750 photographs have been reproduced, amply illustrating so many facets of the town and local life between 1900 and 2000. Nonetheless, despite the wealth of photographs that capture Thetford and its inhabitants at different periods throughout the twentieth century, it is evident that some parts of the town, individual buildings and local events appear to have escaped the attention of photographers, if not that of commentators and historians.

Although *Thetford A Century Remembered* is a photographic record of twentieth century life, inevitably, it captures the remnants and evidence of earlier centuries that have provided a permanent mark on the town, places such as the Cluniac Priory, Castle Hill, St Peter's Church and Town Bridge, for example. While these monuments to an earlier past have survived the twentieth century, numerous buildings in the town were less fortunate and were demolished, eradicated forever! Those of us who value and are interested in Thetford's history are fortunate that some of these buildings were photographed at different periods during the century. These images are very important and valuable documents in that, very often, they are the only visual evidence we have that these buildings ever existed at all.

For the first five decades of the century, Thetford was a small, market town of less than 5,000 inhabitants. It was an intriguing mixture of houses, shops, public houses, churches, chapels, industrial premises and open spaces that had evolved over several centuries. However, once Thetford Borough Council took the decision, after much discussion, that Thetford would become one of a number of London 'overspill' towns, much of this earlier townscape was completely swept away, changing the character of the town. Thetford's industrial activity, such as it was, in and around the core of the old town gradually disappeared, generally, to make way for new shops and car parks. New housing and industrial estates were planned and built around the edge of the quickly expanding town. By the end of the century, Thetford's population had more than quadrupled and 'London' accents outnumbered those of Norfolk.

Clearly, the twentieth century was an eventful period, one of considerable change and progress for the once 'sleepy' Norfolk town of Thetford. As each decade of the twentieth century progressed, it brought new things, values and expectations. At the same time, once familiar objects, fashions and ways disappeared, sometimes rapidly and, at times, so slowly or peaceably that their loss was scarcely noticed. There is hardly a sphere of local life that was not touched by twentieth century progress, inevitably creating a town, and arguably its inhabitants, of a completely different character.

Even though we may have walked the same streets and shared the same experiences and events, all of us, young and old, will have different memories of Thetford. Hopefully, *Thetford A Century Remembered* will have not only evoked many memories but also helped to preserve them. Finally, it is hoped that *Thetford A Century Remembered* will also serve as a valuable source of reference for future Thetfordians.

David Osborne, Thetford, 2010

THE GUILDHALL and MARKET PLACE

'The installation of public baths in the Town Hall is surely a boon to a town like Thetford, ill-supplied with modern arrangements in the dwellings'. Thetford & Watton Times, 7 May 1921

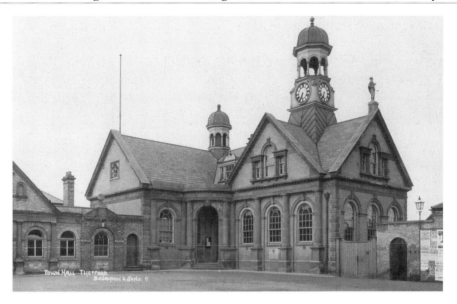

THE GUILDHALL, c.1910

    The Guild or Town Hall was opened in 1902, replacing the Guildhall that had been erected a century earlier. The Guildhall served as the offices and chambers of the Corporation and Borough of Thetford until 1952, when the King's House took on this role. Moreover, throughout the 20th century the Guildhall has been used for numerous civic, public and private events. Perhaps one of its least known functions was as a public bath, located in the basement, for local householders who had no bath facilities.

    As each second of time passed during the 20th century, the Guildhall clock recorded most, if not all, of it. It did cease to function on several occasions, not least of all, when its mechanical parts were removed and replaced with an electric motor in 1972.

THE RED LION, MARKET PLACE, c.1905

    The Corporation of Thetford and, more recently, Thetford Town Council, have owned the Red Lion since a house of that name was first purchased by the Corporation in the 17th century. When this photograph was taken by local photographer Roger Bantock in the early years of the 20th century, the Red Lion was a commercial hotel in the tenancy of Mrs Henrietta Pye, who also operated a posting establishment for the hire of horses and carriages. Thetford's Market Day was then only held on a Saturday. An additional Tuesday market was introduced in 1970, replacing a small Wednesday market.

THE MARKET PLACE, 1910

Besides being an open space for market traders to sell their goods and wares on the prescribed market days, the Market Place has been the scene of all sorts of events throughout the century. Once again, local photographer Roger Bantock captures the Market Place, this time crowded with Thetfordians eager to hear the Mayor, Robert Tilley, read the Proclamation of King George V in May 1910. The Coronation was in August the following year.

THE MARKET PLACE, c.1935

The War Memorial was erected by public subscription and unveiled on the 4th December 1921, "*In ever grateful remembrance of the men of this borough who gave their lives in the Great War 'Lest We forget'.*" In 1948 a ceremony was held to dedicate a panel with the names of those servicemen killed in World War II.

Since 1925, when it was suggested that the Market Place be levelled and covered with tarmac, it has officially been designated as a car park. Certainly, during the 20th century, the general appearance of the Market Place has changed several times. The last major change was in the mid-1980s when the Shambles was converted into retail units and 'Victorian' street furniture was introduced.

THE MARKET PLACE, 1936

Thetford's Boy Scouts and Cubs parade for the Proclamation of King Edward VIII in January 1936. The building standing behind the Scouts and the parked motor vehicle was erected as a Mechanics Institute in 1887, a memorial to Queen Victoria's Jubilee. It ceased to be used as a Mechanics Institute in 1935, when it began a new lease of life as offices for the Corporation. From 1952 until 1970, it served as the Thetford County Library. The new County Library opened in Raymond Street in 1970. Since then the old Mechanics Institute has been a doctors' surgery, wine bar and the local headquarters of the Royal British Legion.

THE MARKET PLACE, 1953

Girls from Thetford Grammar School and the County Primary School, Norwich Road dance before a large crowd gathered on the Market Place. This was part of Thetford's celebrations for the Coronation of Queen Elizabeth in June 1953. The dancing display should have taken place on Coronation Day, the previous week, but as the weather was so wet Thetford's celebrations were curtailed. Other Coronation celebration events included a competition for the best decorated motor vehicle. One entrant was a vehicle covered with pots, pans and other paraphernalia. It carried two threadbare 'Cockneys' bearing a sign *'First of London's Overspill'*.

THE MARKET PLACE, 1996

It is evident from contemporary photographs taken in the early years of the century that some market days appear to have attracted only a few stall holders. The market certainly flourished after the 1939-45 War, when a Wednesday market was established in addition to the ancient chartered market that had been held from time immemorial on Saturdays. As the town's population expanded during the 1960s, the popularity of the market increased, while stallholders asked for the Wednesday market to be moved to another day. At the time, Wednesday was Thetford's 'early closing' day. In 1970, they had their wish when the Wednesday market was abolished and replaced by a Tuesday market. By the end of the century, there were obvious commercial developments that were likely to threaten the economic value of Thetford's market place, such as the appearance of large supermarkets and other retail outlets on the edge of town, and the introduction of new Sunday trading laws in 1994.

REMEMBRANCE DAY, MARKET PLACE, 1984

Mr Richard Easten leads the Remembrance Day parade from the Market Place. The Great War 1914-18 ended when an armistice was agreed on the 11th November. Each year since then, a special service has been held in the town, initially, to honour those local service personnel killed in the Great War but also later conflicts. In 1946, once the hostilities of World War II ceased, Armistice Day became known as Remembrance Day.

THE MARKET PLACE, c.1955

When this photograph was taken the surfaces of the roads around the Market Place and elsewhere in the town were patterned with fresh tarmac, laid down over trenches that were dug for the installation of Thetford's first proper sewage system that began to be implemented in 1949. Even so, there were many households not connected to the sewage system for many years to come.

The gentleman wearing the white apron is Mr Walter Dorling, returning to his place of work behind the counter at Savage Bros, King Street, one of Thetford's best known shops from the early years of the century until closure in 1962. [Photograph courtesy of Studio Five, Thetford]

THE MARKET PLACE, c.1955

Although it is arguable, when Mr Roy Cotterell was 'landlord' of the Green Dragon public house in the 1950s, local life flowed at a much more leisurely pace compared with today. Until 1948 there was a public weighbridge in the road immediately in front of the Dragon. The raised island in the centre of the road became Thetford's first traffic round-about after being enlarged and modified in 1959. [Photograph courtesy of Studio Five, Thetford]

THE MARKET PLACE, c.1910

When this photograph was published on a picture postcard in the early years of the century, the large, ivy-clad house was the residence of Thetford's Medical Officer of Health, Dr A. Harris. By 1922 it was known as the Central Temperance Hotel. Next-door is the Angel public house. Throughout the 20th century and for many years before, an angel, a lion and a dragon have watched over the Market Place. They will have witnessed the numerous events that have taken place on the Market Place, including some amusing ones such as the rivalry that ensued in April 1914, when the organ music of a travelling show competed at the same time with a local band, most probably the Salvation Army, playing hymns.

THE MARKET PLACE, 1984

From the early years of the 20th century, there appears to have been at least one shop situated in this part of the Market Place. From the mid-1930s, butcher, R. Roper and then E.W. Roper traded from number 9 Market Place. Roper's former shop is the one occupied by Norfolk Kitchen that opened in 1972, next-door to the Big Fry fish & chip shop that opened the previous year. By then, these premises formed a part of Guildhall Street. Perhaps the first fish & chip shop to open in Guildhall Street and possibly in the town, was that opened by former Burrell employee George Lambert in 1921.

GUILDHALL STREET and OLD MARKET STREET

'Another of the streets leading from the Market Place is Guildhall Street, termed until a few decades ago Heathenman Street.' W.G. Clarke, *'Guide to the Borough of Thetford'*, published 1923

GUILDHALL STREET, c.1910

Like many other parts of the town centre, Guildhall Street changed very little in the first half of the century. By the end of the century, however, it was almost unrecognizable from that just fifty years earlier. The building on the right, behind the iron railings, is the Primitive Methodist Chapel that was built in the mid-1860s. It ceased as a chapel in 1933 and soon afterwards was opened as a public hall, known as the Central Hall. However, it was demolished in the mid-1960s to make way for the Red Cross building that opened in 1967.

GUILDHALL STREET, 1974

This view from the old junction with Pike Lane looks towards the Market Place. The derelict house on the left is Point House that stood at the junction of Guildhall Street and Raymond Street until demolition in the late 1970s, about the same time as the adjacent properties standing in Guildhall Street. It was 1989, however, before the former Co-op store, a local land-mark for over a century, disappeared from further along the street. Note the very old, possibly medieval doorway adjacent to Point House.

OLD MARKET STREET, 1975

As the name implies, Old Market Street was once Thetford's market place. It ceased as a market place in 1786. Standing on the left is part of the former brewhouse of Bidwell & Co. It was the last local brewery to survive, until its closure in 1924, so ending Thetford's very old brewing tradition. Adjacent is another old building once associated with Bidwell's brewery. In the early 1970s it was being used as a bus garage by the Eastern Counties Omnibus Co. A double-decker bus can be seen parked outside. Underneath this building is a huge cellar with a vaulted ceiling, where barrels of Bidwell's beer were once stored.

Certainly since the 1960s, Bidwell's former brewery has been utilized by a number of different industrial and commercial enterprises.

OLD MARKET STREET, 1975

In the 1930s and early 40s, the single storey building on the right was the dairy premises of Robert Stevenson who also traded from the adjoining shop, with the bow-fronted window, further along the street. Stevenson's dairy business closed in 1944 and, soon after, it became the dairy of B.A. Smith. The old shop front survives but the old dairy was demolished in 1983 to make way for new houses.

CASTLE STREET

'Castle Street is a fine broad thoroughfare leading from the Market Place to Melford Common, Melford Bridge over the River Thet, and Thetford Bridge Station'. Guide to Thetford Norfolk, published 1938

CASTLE STREET, c.1905

From photographs such as this, it is clear to see that very few, if any, of Thetford's roads and streets had a tarmac surface in the early years of the century. The little shop on the left is Lambert's cycle and pram showroom. Later, further along the street, Lambert's had a large garage and coachworks. Modern residences now occupy the site. Nearby, opposite the cycle showroom, is the Three Hoops public house, then the only one in the town tied to Norwich brewer Bullard. By the time the Three Hoops closed in 1930, Bullard owned most of the town's pubs, having taken over Thetford brewer Bidwell & Co.

CASTLE STREET, 1972

November 1972 and Lambert's former cycle & pram showroom at number 15 Castle Street is in a dilapidated condition, waiting to be demolished to make way for The Link, a new road linking Castle Street and Magdalen Street. For the last few years of its existence, 15 Castle Street was the premises of boot & shoe repairer, B. Sturman, before moving his business, as the notice in the window indicates, to 13 Earls Street.

LAMBERT'S GARAGE, CASTLE STREET, 1925

In May 1925, the 250,000th motor car manufactured at Ford's Trafford Works, Manchester visited Thetford. It was photographed on the Market Place and alongside other locally owned Ford motor vehicles outside Lambert's Castle Street garage. W. Lambert began trading in Castle Street in the very early years of the century, but opposite from where they became well established.

In the 1920s Lambert's were busy manufacturing coach and bodyworks for charabancs and in 1925 opened a branch garage on the Norwich Road. About the same time, another local firm, Edmonds Motors of Norton House, Croxton Road, was also manufacturing bodies for motor vehicles and in the summer months operated a popular motor-brake or charabanc service to Yarmouth.

CASTLE STREET, c.1958

By the time that the well known Green's Works Band of Brandon marched along Castle Street in the mid-1950s, motoring had progressed enormously since the Motor Car Act 1903 first introduced vehicle number plates, a speed limit of 20 mph and provision for a driving licence. Even so, local authorities could still enforce a 10 mph limit within the jurisdiction of their cities and towns. Lambert's was still trading in 1960, when the Ministry of Transport introduced a MOT test for vehicles ten years old or more. Eight years later, however, the controlling interest of the Castle Street garage was taken over by a Norwich company Duff Morgan & Vermont Ltd. In 1973, the Castle Garage as it was then known was taken over by Lloyd Baker [Thetford] Ltd.

CASTLE STREET, c.1905

Castle Street has always been a mixture of residential and commercial properties. One business located there early in the century was fish, fruit and game merchant, Harry Goddard, who processed fresh herring from Yarmouth and Lowestoft at his fish curing house in Castle Street. Early in the century Harry Goddard traded from a shop in Magdalen Street before moving to the Market Place about 1917. He also sold bloaters, kippers and other produce from horse-drawn carts, before changing to a motor van.

CASTLE STREET, c.1905

The site of Harry Goddard's curing house was next door to the light coloured house standing on the left, number 38. In 1908 the site became occupied, for many years, by the premises of ironmonger, Frank Clarke.

CASTLE STREET, 1986

Frank Clarke's shop and premises were badly damaged by a fire in 1973. It was refurbished and finally demolished to make way for Rampart Way, a new road linking Castle Street with Raymond Street that opened in 1991.

MELFORD BRIDGE ROAD, c.1925

Well before the end of the 20th century, what was earlier known as Coronation Avenue and then Melford Bridge Road became the east end of Castle Street. Until June 1953 when passenger trains ceased passing through Thetford's Bridge Station, Melford Bridge Road, as it was still called, formed an attractive avenue to and from the station. The avenue of Horse Chestnut trees was planted to commemorate the Coronation of King Edward VII in 1902.

THE MELFORD BRIDGE and BRIDGE TAVERN, c.1912

The Bridge Tavern was built and opened about the same time as the Bridge Station in 1876. The railway station, hidden from view behind the Bridge Tavern, was situated in the neighbouring parish of Brettenham and Snarehill. Once you passed over the Melford Bridge and the River Thet you were officially outside the Borough of Thetford. This photograph was probably taken in August 1912 when Thetford and other parts of Norfolk experienced extensive flooding after several hours of torrential rain.

The Bridge Tavern was renamed 'Flints' in 1984 and then 'The Bridge' in 1992.

THE CASTLE HILL and PARK

'A castle was built at Thetford, almost certainly in the period 1067-69 immediately after the Conquest and simultaneously with the first castle at Norwich'.
Alan Crosby, *'A History of Thetford'*, published 1986

CASTLE HILL, 1944

This photograph was taken by an unknown American serviceman during the war and captures the man-made Castle Hill, overgrown with vegetation and in a much more natural state than we are used to seeing. Obviously, during the war there was much more important work to be done. For Thetford's children during the 1939-45 War, however, the Castle Hill and Park was an ideal haven for games such as hide and seek or pretending to be soldiers engaged in modern warfare.

CASTLE HILL, 1996

Even during the 20th century, the Castle Hill's origins and history have been the subject of much conjecture. In the early 1960's, archaeological excavations on the hill and outer ramparts revealed evidence of an Iron Age fortification dating from about 500 BC. These early defences were later incorporated into the Norman 'motte' and bailey we see today. If there was a castle on the summit, it was most likely a wooden structure as no evidence of stonework was found.

The Castle Hill has a place in local folklore although much of this has little relevance or meaning in the 20th century. One story tells that the hill was constructed by the Devil shaking dirt from his cloven foot. Another story relates that six silver bells, taken from Thetford's Cluniac priory, are buried under the hill.

CASTLE PARK, 1908

Thetford's Castle meadow was opened as a public park by Lady William Cecil, the daughter of Lord and Lady Amherst of nearby Didlington Hall, on the 5th September 1908. The Amherst's owned most of the Castle Hill and the meadow but leased it to the Corporation of Thetford for 99 years, at a nominal annual rent of £1 per annum. In 1921, however, the Corporation purchased the freehold for £25.

CASTLE PARK, c.1954

Besides the numerous unofficial contests involving cricket, football, rounders and the like, the Castle Park was the venue for numerous events during the 20th century, including those organised to raise funds for the Cottage Hospital, before the National Health Service was formed in 1948.

In 1961, close to where these boys are playing, a large pond suitable for small children in which to paddle in or sail model yachts and boats on, was constructed to commemorate the centenary of the Thetford Co-operative Society. In 1975, the pond was turned into a children's sand pit but this has since disappeared. [Photograph courtesy of 'Billy' Filby]

CASTLE PARK, 1975

A special play area for children and playing apparatus was first created in 1935, to commemorate the Silver Jubilee of King George V. A drinking water fountain, that now stands near the Mill Head, was also erected at the same time as a Jubilee Memorial. Since then various children's play equipment such as swings, slides, roundabouts, see-saws and climbing apparatus have been erected and replaced at different times.

THE BRIDGE STATION

'There is a considerable goods traffic, but passenger bookings have been extremely light'.
'Branch Lines To Thetford', *The Railway Magazine,* published June 1953

THE BRIDGE STATION, c.1935

Thetford Bridge Station was built in the mid-1870s when the railway branch line between Thetford and Bury St Edmunds was opened. Besides the passenger station there was also a signal box, several sidings, a goods shed and yard. In the 1950s, just before the passenger service ceased in 1953, there were four passenger trains daily in each direction on weekdays and an additional passenger train in each direction on Saturdays. Perhaps the busiest time at the Bridge Station was during both World Wars when the line was used extensively for transporting military goods and personnel to nearby camps. The railway employee on the station platform, wearing the peaked cap, is most likely the station master Mr F. Goddard.

THETFORD BRIDGE YOUTH HOSTEL, c.1960

After the loss of the passenger service between Thetford and Bury St Edmunds in 1953, the Bridge Station was effectively closed to passengers. However, the Bridge Station opened as a Youth Hostel, run by the YHA, in 1955 and it continued until closure in 1971. Furthermore, after the end of the passenger service, a daily goods train, known affectionately as the 'Bury Rattler', continued to operate until June 1960. Soon afterwards the railway track was completely removed.

THE BRIDGE STATION, 1972

Within a few months of the Thetford Bridge Youth Hostel closing, the once well-kept platform and station buildings appear to have become a storage space for an assortment of motor vehicles, other goods and materials.

Although the A11–A134 link via the Mundford Road was opened in 1973, it was December 1975 before the southern part of the link road, the route of the former Bury–Thetford railway, was opened to motor traffic. This road is now known as Hurth Way, linking the A1066 and A1088 with the Norwich Road. Thetford has both civic and cultural links with the German town of Hurth.

THE MELFORD BRIDGE and COMMON

'In 1937 it was agreed that the use of the Melford Common pits, a dumping ground for centuries, should be terminated because of the proximity of houses'. Alan Crosby, *'A History of Thetford'*, published 1986

MELFORD BRIDGE, 1997

Melford Bridge was built in 1697, by Sir John Wodehouse, whose Arms can still be seen displayed on the bridge. The name 'Melford' is derived from 'millford', implying that there was once a mill and a forded river crossing, presumably, close to where the Melford Bridge now stands over the river Thet. The Thet has its source in the Attleborough area where several streams merge.

For much of the century the river, close to the old Melford Bridge, has been a popular resort for children to paddle and play, even after a modern, indoor swimming pool was opened on the Croxton Road in 1972 at a reported cost of £170,000.

MELFORD TERRACE. THETFORD. 134.

MELFORD TERRACE, MELFORD BRIDGE ROAD, c.1915

The flint cottages on the left were probably built in the 18th century, well before Melford Terrace was built on the edge of the Melford Common in the early years of the 20th century. Apparently, Melford Terrace was soon nick-named "Honeymoon Terrace" as so many newly-weds lived there. In the early years of the 20th century, from the front of their houses they would have looked out and across to a truly rural scene, common and agricultural land bisected, in the middle distance, by a railway line. Later residents, in the late 1950s and early 60s, witnessed the building of numerous houses and bungalows to create Norfolk Road and the Redgate Estate.

MELFORD COMMON, 1993

For centuries the Melford Common has been a venue for all sorts of events. During the 20th century, after parts of the Melford Common ceased to be used as a general dumping ground for all sorts of household and industrial waste, the common has been the scene of numerous events, annual bonfires and regular visits from travelling amusement fairs and circuses. In earlier times travelling fairs set-up their rides and stalls on the Market Place.

MELFORD COMMON, 1993

In the 18th century, criminals were executed at gallows erected on the Melford Common. The cottages in the background were built on a piece of ground once known as 'Gallows Close'. Well into the 1950s, there was still evidence of the rubbish pits that were a feature earlier in the 20th century.

This display of horsemanship is performed by the Household Cavalry who were training at nearby Stanford.

MELFORD COMMON, 1999

In 1999 Thetford celebrated 800 years of Mayoralty with a visit from HRH the Prince of Wales. Other events included a pageant and music concerts, including a performance by the famous jazz musician Humphrey Lyttleton and his band. Unfortunately, the weather on the evening of the jazz concert was wet and cold, which deterred some people from attending. The previous evening, however, it was warm and dry as hundreds of Thetfordians enjoyed the music of the Beatles performed by a popular tribute band known as the Bootleg Beatles.

MAGDALEN STREET

'Besides its interesting shape, Magdalen Street is lined with an interesting mixture of buildings which reflect the diversity of Thetford's past and present society'. David Osborne, *'Thetford Gleanings'*, published 2003

MAGDALEN STREET, c.1953

This end of Magdalen Street, nearest the Market Place, has always boasted several shops and other commercial premises. By the early 1930s, Wilfred Pearson had taken over the bakery of William Marshall at number 2, while opposite at number 1, L.D. Barnetson began selling wireless supplies. Once television began being transmitted from nearby Tacolneston early in 1955, Barnetson's shop was one of several busy supplying TV sets to local homes. On the corner of Earls Street was Doran's toy and chinaware shop that closed in the early 1970s and is now appropriately named Doran's Corner.

YMCA, MAGDALEN STREET, 1912

In 1905 the Young Men's Christian Association opened premises in White Hart Street. Besides bible reading classes, members were soon enjoying facilities such as a miniature rifle range and the use of a bathroom. At that time many local homes did not have the luxury of a bathroom.

The first president of the Thetford YMCA was Josiah Vavasseur of Kilverstone Hall, who on his death in 1908, bequeathed a plot of freehold land in Magdalen Street and a sum of money to build a new YMCA hall. The handsome new building was opened in 1912, by Mr R.L. Barclay MA, Honorary Treasurer of the National YMCA. During both of the World Wars, Thetford's YMCA provided numerous facilities for the comfort and recreation of thousands of airmen and troops stationed in the area.

MAGDALEN STREET, c.1912

Magdalen Street is still easily recognizable, despite some changes to its appearance since the early years of the 20th century. The single storey building on the left was the premises of monumental stonemason, Robert Hall, who was also Captain of the Borough of Thetford Fire Brigade. On the opposite side of the road a milkman's handcart can been seen. In those days milk wasn't delivered from the dairy in bottles but was ladled or poured from a milk churn into a variety of containers provided by the householders.

In 1973, residents from Magdalen Street and Melford Bridge Road were busy campaigning and protesting against heavy goods vehicles using this part of the old town as a main route through Thetford. They even formed a human barricade across the street near the Black Horse public house to disrupt the flow of motor traffic.

HARBORD ALMSHOUSES, MAGDALEN STREET, 1975

Local charities continued to have an important role in 20th century life, even though they may have been established many years earlier. These almshouses were founded in the late 17th century by William Harbord MP for Thetford. They were originally built for six poor men. William Harbord's father, Sir Charles Harbord was also a generous benefactor to the town. The Harbord Almshouses were modernized several times during the 20th century by Thetford Municipal Charities, the body responsible for their management and maintenance.

EARLS STREET

'Earls Street, formerly known as Earls Lane – a street name which in this context assumes a great significance for it presumably relates to the Earls Warren, lords of the Manor'.
Alan Crosby, *'A History of Thetford'*, published 1986

EARLS STREET, c.1960

Earls Street was once commonly known as Alice's Lane but by the middle of the 19th century it was Earls Lane. In the very early years of the 20th century most of the houses standing in Earls Street were at the end towards the Market Place. By the end of the century, however, there were very few vacant or suitable building plots to be found in Earls Street.

The terraced houses and a fish and chip shop, on the right, were demolished in the early 1970s to create parking space and access to the rear of the Post Office. [Photograph courtesy of Thetford Town Council]

CONGREGATIONAL CHURCH, EARLS STREET, c.1910

Since it was built in the first quarter of the 19th century, as a Meeting House for Thetford's Independents, it has undergone numerous changes. After a meeting in January, 1902, it became a United Congregational Church and later that year the building was renovated at a cost of £46 10s 0d while a sum of £42 5s 9d was raised at a Church bazaar. Later, in 1972 it became a United Reform Church by the union of the Congregational Church and the Presbyterian Church in England.

Like other churches in the town during the 1939-45 War, evening services had to be reorganized so as not to infringe the stringent 'Black-Out' regulations.

CONGREGATIONAL CHURCH, EARLS STREET, c.1910

The organ, on the left, was installed in 1910, having been removed from Thetford's St Cuthbert's Church. Its arrival caused some alterations to be made to the interior. Afterwards, however, the interior remained virtually unchanged until 1998, when major renovations swept away the old pulpit, pews and fittings, and the old and valuable organ was reinstalled in a new position, on the opposite side of the church. The new work created a light, spacious interior, a place of worship readily adapted for many secular uses.

ODDFELLOWS HALL, EARLS STREET, 1999

The Oddfellows, Thetford's biggest benefit society well into the 20th century, had this hall built as their headquarters. Besides, the hall has had many uses. Before and during the 1914-18 War, it was also used as a cinema. It has also been the venue for numerous theatrical and music concerts including those performed by ENSA [Entertainments National Service Association] to boost morale during the dark and uncertain years of the 1939-45 War.

By 1946, however, the Oddfellows appear to have vacated the hall as it had become known as Breckland Hall, a venue for all sorts of private and public meetings and events.

From the mid-1950s until 1965, it was the factory premises of electronic components manufacturer, Cathodeon Ltd, and then a new company known as Harvey Hall, which continued producing and assembling electronic components in the former Oddfellows Hall for a few more years. Since 1985 it has been the Thetford Snooker Centre.

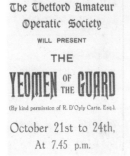

The Thetford Amateur Operatic Society

WILL PRESENT

THE

YEOMEN OF THE GUARD

(By kind permission of R. D'Oyly Carte, Esq.).

October 21st to 24th, At 7.45 p.m.

AT THE

ODDFELLOWS' HALL, THETFORD.

SEATS 3/-, 2/-, 1/-.

May be Reserved at Messrs. H. Green's, King Street, Thetford.

Proceeds to

Thetford Cottage Hospital.

EARLS STREET, c.1925

All the cottages seen in this photograph survived into the late 20th century, even if the interiors and uses changed along with ownership. The signboard of the Globe beerhouse has certainly gone and the house is now a private residence. Opposite is Foresters Row, erected in 1909 by the Ancient Order of Foresters, one of Thetford's benefit societies. It is worth noting the large poles carrying the town's electricity supplies and telephone cables. Although they are no longer to be seen in Earls Street, they continue to be a feature in some parts of the town.

EARLS STREET, c.1910

Pedestrian pavements were laid in some parts of the town as early as the 1790s but photographs taken in the first two decades of the 20th century illustrate that at least some parts of Earl Street were still devoid of such refinements. In the 1930s, the flint and chalk wall on the left was demolished to make way for the construction of Thetford's first ambulance station. A Norfolk Constabulary Police house was erected on the opposite side of the road in the 1950s.

THE AMBULANCE STATION, EARLS STREET, c.1938

Volunteer members of Thetford's St John Ambulance brigade stand outside the Ambulance Station that was opened in 1938, to commemorate the Coronation of King George VI the previous year. The Thetford Brigade was formed by Sir William Gentle in 1937 to provide trained first-aid personnel, primarily to support the local ambulance service and also at other times when needed in the town and district.

THE AMBULANCE STATION, EARLS STREET, 1995

Thetford never owned a motor ambulance until 1921, when the Thetford Borough Council purchased an old, second-hand ambulance for the town. By 1924 it had become so unreliable and uneconomic that it was disposed of and the Council made an agreement with nearby Attleborough to share their motor ambulance when needed and if available. Eventually, in 1937 two generous benefactors, Miss Emily Fison and her sister, Mrs Katherine Mason, purchased a brand-new motor ambulance for the use of the town. Moreover, a small plot of land in Earls Street was given by local butcher, George Reeve, for the construction of an ambulance station, financed through public subscription as a Coronation memorial.

The Ambulance Station became redundant in 1971 when a new one was erected and opened on Croxton Road [now Old Croxton Road]. The former Ambulance Station is managed and maintained by Thetford Municipal Charities.

NORWICH ROAD and LIME KILN LANE

NORWICH ROAD, 1984

A branch garage of G.W. Lambert was built on this site and opened in 1924. In the 1950s, petrol continued to be dispensed from pumps that stood against the garage and beside the pavement so that, when vehicles were being filled, pedestrians had to manoeuvre around the hose dispensing the fuel. Moreover, perhaps some of these pedestrians were even smoking. Lambert's old garage closed in 1967 but was soon replaced by this modern Shell petrol service station known as The Chase. Until the by-pass opened in 1989, this was the busy A11 trunk road through the town. It is now the A1075.

THETFORD POLICE STATION, NORWICH ROAD, 1944

The Norwich Road Police Station and adjoining inspector's house was opened in 1936, replacing the Police Station at the Old Gaol, Old Market Street. When this photograph was taken, brick walls had been built to protect the front entrance from the possible effects of exploding bombs, if dropped from enemy aircraft. During the 1939-45 War many public and municipal buildings were protected this way or with sand bags. In 1962 work began building a new extension to the existing building and in the early 1970s a new and much larger Police Station was built on the site. Other extensions have been added since then and all that survives of the original Police Station is part of the perimeter wall.

LIME KILN LANE, 1988

For many decades before the 20th century, lime burning was carried out in this part of the town. Once the local lime industry ceased, this area became agricultural land - a small holding. One or two modern bungalows were built in Lime Kiln Lane in the 1960s but things changed rapidly in the late 1980s when hedges, shrubbery and a bungalow were cleared away for a small, residential development.

LIME KILN LANE, 1991

For many years in the 20th century, certainly until the 1960s, Lime Kiln Lane was a narrow, hedge-lined, back road on the edge of the town. Within a few years it changed to a busy commercial and residential area of a greatly expanded town. In 1967, motor mechanic, Stefan Zurowski, began motor repairs from this site, an old building that had stood there for many years. After Stefan retired in 1991, the business was continued by his son Paul. [Photograph courtesy of Stefan Zurowski]

LIME KILN LANE, 1996

This photograph was taken from the Norwich Road as industrial and retail buildings, erected in the late 1960s and early 70s, were being demolished for a new phase of development. Previously this area was one large, open pit once associated with the local lime burning industry. Businesses occupying this site in the early 1980s included the Central Tyre Company, Robert Lee [London] Ltd, Thetford Garden Centre and Wyatt Builders Merchants.

LIME KILN LANE, 1998

The second phase of development of the Thetford Retail Park began with the clearance of the previous buildings and then the construction of the Aldi supermarket that opened in 1998, on the site previously occupied by Thetford Garden Centre.

In the background, new retail units are being constructed on land behind properties lining the west side of Magdalen Street.

NORWICH ROAD, c.1910

The house in the foreground is Glebe House, standing on the corner of Vicarage Road. When it was built as a vicarage for the incumbent of St Cuthbert's Church in the 1880s, Vicarage Road did not exist. Even in the early years of the 20th century, when this photograph was taken, Glebe House was still very much on the outskirts of the town. Beyond can be seen new houses built opposite the Ark beerhouse and a bridge carrying the Norwich Road over the Thetford – Bury St Edmunds railway.

THE ARK, NORWICH ROAD, c.1950

Originally a farm house and beerhouse, by the early 1950s the Ark was one of 16 public houses in the town. Although well away from the town centre the tenant and licensee could guarantee a good passing trade from travellers on the Norwich Road, particularly from day trippers in the summer months, as they made their way through the town by car, coach and motor cycle to the popular resort of Great Yarmouth and other coastal towns. In the mid-1950s the Ark was a popular venue for 'Talent Nights' that encouraged local people to perform as entertainers in front of an audience.

NORWICH ROAD, 1967

This road bridge carrying the A11 over the Bury–Thetford railway was demolished soon after this photograph was taken. Where the old bridge once stood, a new traffic roundabout was built, linking a new section of the Mundford Road to the A11 that was opened in 1972. In 1975, the project was completed when the southern section was built along the route of the former Thetford – Bury railway, joining the A11 at the Norwich Road roundabout; this is now called Hurth Way. By the late 1960s, new housing estates were being built on land between the Norwich Road and the Thetford – Norwich railway. [Photograph courtesy of Thetford Town Council]

J. BOARDMAN'S PETROL STATION, NORWICH ROAD, c.1938

As the number of motor vehicles on local roads increased during the 1920s and 30s, so did the number of different businesses and enterprises to cater for the needs of the motorist. About 1932, J. Boardman established a petrol service station outside the front of his house at number 87 Norwich Road and traded from there until the mid-1940s. The petrol pumps were manually operated by the action of a handle being pumped up and down. Thetford's very first self-service petrol station opened just a few yards further north along the Norwich Road in 1971. [Photograph courtesy of John Alvey]

CROXTON ROAD and VICARAGE ROAD

'The Croxton Road was once a popular walk for many Thetfordians. They would head out of the town and out along the hedge-lined Croxton Road, before turning right into Joe Blunt's Lane, passing Lord Fisher's blackcurrant fields, along the lane and onto the Norwich Road.'
Daphne Burlingham, *'All In A Life Time',* published 2001

CROXTON ROAD, c.1905

Until the mid-1970s, Croxton Road was not only the main route to Croxton but also Mundford and Kings Lynn. Certainly in the early years of the 20th century and, for a few decades later, it was still fairly safe for children to play games and loiter on the highway without too much risk of being run over by a passing vehicle, be it horse-drawn or motorized. For pedestrians and cyclists, in particular, the journey from the bottom of White Hart Street to the top of Croxton Road could be a long and tiring haul, especially on a windy day.

The cottages in the right foreground were later demolished to make way for the garage premises of H.R. & D.E. Doran.

H.R. & D.E. DORAN, CROXTON ROAD, c.1930

Harold Doran and his brother Derek established this garage on Croxton Road [now Old Croxton Road] in 1926. Other garage proprietors and motor engineers in Thetford at the same time were C.R. & C.H. Allison of White Hart Street; Hanbury & Co of London Road; W. & G. Lambert of Castle Street and Norwich Road, and W.J. Woods Ltd of Bridge Street. [Photograph courtesy of John Alvey]

CROXTON ROAD, 1975

These flint cottages, numbers 18 and 20, were demolished in March 1988. The cottage on the left, number 20, was a 19th century beerhouse called the 'Plough'. For a few years in the 1930s & 40s, it was the grocery shop of Percy Green. By the time this photograph was taken, Doran's old garage had been replaced by a modern garage and service station, the premises of Croxton Motors. The garage was demolished about the same time as the cottages and is now occupied by Summer Court and Crown House Close.

COACH SERVICES, DORAN'S YARD, CROXTON ROAD, c.1955

Throughout the 20th century this was known locally as Doran's Yard, where Thomas Doran's steam contracting business was established in the 1890s and continued to operate from Croxton Road until the late-1950s, when steam powered road rollers finally ceased to be used for repairing local roads. Obsolete steam rollers and other equipment, such as the Burrell-built living van in the picture, then stood abandoned and neglected in Doran's Yard for several years. Thomas Doran's son Derek purchased his first motor coach in 1929 and later established Coach Services [1947]. Although he sold the business in 1969, Coach Services continued to operate from Doran's Yard, Croxton Road at the very end of the 20th century.

CROXTON ROAD, c.1910

These houses were built privately between the later years of the 19th century and early years of the 20th, providing comfortable, modern homes, generally, for local middle-class families. Frederick W. Doran, Burrell's chief draughtsman, built number 23 in the early years of the century and lived there for many years while his brother, Thomas R. Doran, lived opposite at Haughley House, Croxton Road. Thetford's long serving Town Clerk, G. R. Blaydon, lived for many years at number 37.

CROXTON ROAD MALTINGS, 1975

These large maltings were being used to produce malt until the 1960s. By 1970, after standing redundant for a few years, they were converted into a factory warehouse by furniture manufacturer Ryman Conran Ltd whose main factory was situated in Stephenson Way. The former maltings were badly damaged by fire in August 1980. Soon afterwards the ruined buildings were demolished and the site cleared. It is now occupied by Ben Culey Drive, a small residential estate named after a local businessman.

CROXTON ROAD, c.1950

There are probably not too many people in the town today who can remember the Croxton Road at the old Mundford Road junction. This view was taken from the railway bridge, looking towards Croxton. Although the bridge is still there, little else is recognizable today. The buildings in the distance form the CSD [Command Stores Depot], a military depot established during the 1939-45 War. It was closed in the late 1990s and the site is now the residential Stanford Close and Richard Easten Road. The Croxton Road bridge was closed to motor traffic in 1973, once a new road was opened linking the A134 Mundford Road and A11 Norwich Road. [Photograph courtesy of Brian Boughton]

VICARAGE ROAD, 1906

The sender of this picture postcard wrote, "Vicarage Road is noted for newly married couples, that's where I'm going to live." Although the road was still unmade and there were no pavements, they would certainly have been attractive, modern houses for any young couple to buy or, most probably, privately rent in the early 1900s. They were certainly a great improvement on the small, flint built cottages found in many parts of the town. By 1950 there were a total of 84 houses and bungalows in Vicarage Road. Since then many more have been built.

STATION ROAD and the RAILWAY STATION

'The railway station, to be found at the north side of the town, stands on the main rail link between Norwich and Cambridge, from where connections can take you to Liverpool Street or any other part of the country.'
Thetford Official Guide, published 1983

STATION ROAD, c.1915

For much of the 19th century this was known as Mundford Road, the main route leading to Two Mile Bottom and the more distant village of Mundford. Once the level crossing and the road over the railway was closed to vehicular traffic in the 1880s, it then became known as Station Road. Throughout the century, several businesses traded from Station Road, including printers, W. Boughton & Sons Ltd. Boughton's electric printing works, seen in the right foreground, was established there in 1897. In the distance, on the left, are the premises of local builder, Samuel Holden & Son.

STATION ROAD, c.1915

The signboard of the Coach & Horses beerhouse can be seen in the distance, one of the few buildings that stood on the Mundford Road before the arrival of the railway in 1845. There were still very few buildings standing in Station Road at the very beginning of the century but by the 1970s there were very few open spaces. These grand looking houses were erected in the late 19th or early years of the 20th century.

STATION ROAD, c.1960

Station Road can be seen at the bottom right corner, going diagonally across the view. The light-coloured roof that can be seen in the centre foreground is a Government or Ministry storage warehouse, erected in the mid-1950s and accessed from a private road that led off from the Station Road. By the time that this photograph was taken, most of the land either side of Station Road had been developed. One of the few open spaces remaining was a large chalk pit, just west of the Station Road, that formed part of the garden of Avenue House, once St Peter's Rectory, standing at the end of St Nicholas Street. [Photograph courtesy of Thetford Town Council]

THETFORD STATION, c.1910

Thetford is on the railway between Norwich Thorpe, Ely and March. By the beginning of the 20th century, the railway station had been an important part of the townscape for over half a century. In 1900, enamel advertising signs adorned the station and gas or oil lamps provided illumination in the hours of darkness. A great attraction for travellers on the station platform until 1971 was W.H. Smith's kiosk or stall, selling newspapers, magazines, cigarettes and other goods.

In 1990, a fire destroyed the roof of the old station building. By then, however, the station's appearance had declined and the railway had lost some of its former importance as a mode for transporting passengers and goods. Eventually, it was announced in 1997, that over £400,000 was to be spent repairing Thetford Station.

THETFORD STATION, c.1910

A steam locomotive approaches the station from the direction of Brandon while another locomotive stands in one of several sidings, west of the station. The white painted fencing in the distance is livestock pens for holding cattle, sheep and other animals in transit. A butcher's slaughter-house was situated nearby. The siding in the left foreground was for more general, non-perishable goods while coal, a major import, and malt, an important export, were generally handled at sidings in the goods yard east of the station.

THETFORD STATION, 1984

Although the cover that adorned the footbridge disappeared in the early years of the century, as did a large water tank that stood upon a large, brick tower to the right of the footbridge, the general appearance of the station has changed very little. Well before the end of the century, the ambiance of the place had changed from one of life and activity to a cold, lifeless, uninspiring sort of place. Certainly until the 1970s, the station was staffed by numerous railway employees. There were clerks who issued tickets to passengers, answered enquires and dealt with small parcels and lost property. Porters assisted passengers, moved goods about the platforms on special trolleys, and loaded and offloaded a variety of goods from each passenger train that stopped at Thetford, besides keeping the station 'spick and span'. In the goods yards, either end of the station, 'shunters' organised the numerous goods wagons in the sidings. And from a small, dark, oily smelling room near the footbridge, the lamp boy ensured that the oil lamps for the signals were maintained and in position.

THETFORD STATION, 1979

A passenger train hauled by a Brush Type 2 locomotive approaches the station from the direction of Norwich. This class of diesel locomotive began working through Thetford in 1957, soon after they were first introduced by British Railways to replace steam locomotives on the Eastern Region.

Thetford's railway sidings were regularly used for loading and off-loading all sorts of goods from coal, malt, timber, steel, machinery, sugar beet and other agricultural produce including livestock. The author remembers standing in this yard in the mid-1950s and watching circus elephants and other animals being off-loaded. By the late-1970s, the sidings were already in the process of being removed. The land was sold to a private developer and building work began in the early 1990s.

THETFORD STATION, 1996

This photograph captures a past railway era as preserved ex-British Railways locomotive 70000 'Britannia' passes at speed through Thetford, on a special steam excursion from Norwich in April 1996. In the 1950s and early 60s locomotives such as this, weighing 94 tons with six 6' 2" diameter driving wheels, were a common and regular sight, hauling a variety of passenger and goods trains through Thetford. The end of the steam era on the Great Eastern lines was commemorated in March 1962, when a special steam-hauled rail tour passed through Thetford, on route between Norwich and Liverpool Street Station, London.

The former sidings and goods yard are occupied by a residential development known as The Sidings and can be seen in the background.

THE WATERWORKS & SEWAGE WORKS

'Beyond the Station is the Mundford Road, and within half a mile are the Municipal Waterworks, opened in 1877. The supply of good water for the town has never failed since that date.'
Guide to Thetford Norfolk, published 1931

THE WATER WORKS, MUNDFORD ROAD, c.1910

Thetfordians relied solely on their water butts, wells and the local rivers for a supply of water before the Corporation Water Works was built on the Mundford Road in 1877. A stationary steam engine, supplied by Walter F. Mason of Ipswich, was installed at the Water Works to pump water from a 160 feet [48 metres] deep bore-hole. This provided the town, for the first time, with a modern, piped water system. Even so, it was many years later before all parts of town were connected to the water mains.

In the 1890s, Charles Burrell & Sons Ltd of the St Nicholas Works, Thetford, supplied a duplicate steam engine, seen above. Steam power was finally replaced at the Water Works when a new engine house was built and two Blackstone crude oil engines installed in 1925. At the same time, the 65 feet [20 metres] high Water Works chimney was demolished. Progress continued when electric pumps were introduced early in 1955. However, the old Blackstone engines were still in situation, perhaps as a standby, in the early 1970s.

The top picture captures Water Works Superintendent, Mr Edward S. Greenwood, who lived with his family at the Water Works House, adjacent to the house containing the pumping machinery.

THE WATER WORKS, 1987

Many schemes have been implemented to keep the town supplied with fresh water since the London 'overspill' was agreed in the 1950s. The very first project completed was the construction of a water pumping station on the edge of Barnham Cross Common to supply a town with a much larger population. This was soon followed in 1960 with the completion of a 1million gallon reservoir at Barrow Hill, just west of the town and in 1966 with the construction of another million gallon reservoir just off the Mundford Road, close to the Victorian Water Works.

The Corporation ceased to be responsible for the town's water in 1973 when Anglian Water Authority took on this responsibility. It is believed that the old Water Works then finally ceased pumping duties but continued as a District Office for the water authority until the end of the century. In 1989 Anglian Water Authority was privatised and became Anglian Water Services.

BOROUGH of THETFORD SEWAGE TREATMENT WORKS, 1970

Thetford was without a proper, modern sewage system until the late 1940s, when work finally began implementing a much needed scheme. It involved the construction of a sewage treatment works west of the town, beside the Little Ouse river, and the laying of sewage mains connecting most, if not all, households throughout the town. Since first operating in the early 1950s the Sewage Works has been extended and modernized several times as the town's population increased. This photograph captures the newly completed 'Phase Two Extensions', officially opened by the Mayor, Councillor T.J. Lamb in July, 1970. [Photograph courtesy of Thetford Town Council]

THE ABBEY

'The Priory of Our Lady of Thetford belonged to the Order of Cluny, and was founded in 1103-4 by Roger Bigod, the old soldier, friend and counsellor of William the Conqueror.'
Department of the Environment Official Handbook, *'Thetford Priory'*, published 1979

THE ABBEY GATE. c.1910

The so-called Abbey Gate was once the main entrance to Thetford's largest and most important religious house, the Cluniac Priory. The priory was dissolved along with so many other religious houses in the middle of the 16th century. Now surrounded by residential homes, the Abbey Gate is the best surviving structure of this once important place.

THE CLUNIAC PRIORY, 1951

Thetford Priory was one of about thirty Cluniac houses, established in England in the 11th and 12th centuries. After the Dissolution, the once grand priory at Thetford quickly became a ruin. For the first three decades of the 20th century, the ruined Cluniac Priory was overgrown with vegetation and generally uncared for. Then, in the mid-1930s, the Ministry of Public Buildings and Works carried out an extensive archaeological excavation besides renovating and preserving the surviving ruins.

This photograph was taken at a special service to commemorate the Festival of Britain in 1951. It is believed to have been the first time that a religious service had taken place there for over 400 years.

THE PRIOR'S LODGINGS, c.1900

When photographed in the early years of the century, the former Prior's Lodgings or House formed part of the private garden of the Abbey House. It is not known exactly when the Prior's Lodgings and garden was separated from the Abbey House and converted back to the Cluniac Priory but was probably about the time that the Ministry of Public Buildings and Works carried out the extensive excavations and restoration.

In 1999 the Prior's Lodgings formed a background to a historic pageant, performed by Thetford's schools, that told the story of Thetford's long and historic past.

CLUNIAC PRIORY & THE ABBEY HUTS, 1944

During the 1939-45 War, thousands of allied troops trained in the Thetford area. Some were accommodated in buildings in the town, such as disused maltings and agricultural buildings. Huts and tents were also erected as temporary billets in various parts of the borough. This rare photograph captures Nissen huts, erected immediately behind the medieval ruins of the Priory Church, where the Abbeygate private residential estate stands today. A tented camp was also erected just south of the Priory ruins, close to the river.

For a few years after the war the 'Abbey Huts', officially known as the 'Abbey Ground', provided temporary, rented accommodation for at least five local families while they waited to be properly housed by Thetford Borough Council.

THE ABBEY HOUSE c.1900

This view captures the Abbey House and Abbeygate when they still formed part of the Abbey Farm. The Abbey Farm was a working farm until the early 1960s, when the farming equipment and stock was sold pending the land being used for a large residential development under the Town Development or 'Overspill' scheme and some private development. Work began constructing the Abbey Farm Estate in 1967.

THE ABBEY HOUSE, c.1910

The Abbey House was built, within the former precincts of the Cluniac Priory, in the early years of the 19th century, most probably for the Steward of the Croxton Manor Estate. Thetford's Cluniac monks once owned the manor of Croxton. In the early years of the 20th century it belonged to the Mackenzie family of Fawley Court, Buckinghamshire and Downham Hall, near Brandon, who also owned the Canon's and Downham Estates.

When the Thetford part of the large, Croxton Estate was broken up and auctioned off in October 1934, the Abbey House and 14 acres of adjoining gardens and grounds were sold by auction and purchased by the Metropolitan Railway Company. Since 1970, the Abbey House has been in private ownership and remains as one of the town's most substantial houses.

ABBEY GREEN, c.1965

Dwellings probably began to be built in this part of the town in the second-half of the 18th century. Most were small, flint cottages and, like the Abbey House, belonged to the Croxton Estate until they were sold, individually in auction, by HM Commissioners for Crown Lands in 1934. Then, the annual rents for these properties were between £6 10s [£6.50] and £10 8s [£10.40].

When these photographs were taken there were 16 dwellings in Abbey Green and in 1972 Thetford Borough Council agreed plans and undertook to renovate thirteen cottages in Abbey Green, to provide seven modern dwellings and also to build six new dwellings in the same style as the old properties. Boughton [Builders] Ltd of Thetford were awarded the construction contract and in August 1974 the work was completed at a reported cost of £115,000. On completion it was planned to sell the dwellings.

There is some evidence that the cottage in the bottom photograph, now number 9 Abbey Green, was originally built as a chapel in the 18th century. [Photographs courtesy of Thetford Town Council]

MINSTERGATE and ST NICHOLAS STREET

'The excavations at St Nicholas Street have demonstrated the presence of Late Saxon occupation on the north bank of the Little Ouse River which, on the basis of the coins and pottery, probably began as early as AD 1000.' Phil Andrews and Kenneth Penn, *'Excavations in Thetford North of the River, 1989-90',* East Anglian Archaeology 87, published 1999

MINSTERGATE, c.1966

The photographer stood at the junction of Water Lane and Abbeygate to capture this view of the Water Lane and Minstergate junction. The gable end of the house in the foreground was once the Duke's Head beerhouse that closed in the 1930s and was demolished soon after this photograph was taken. The house on the opposite corner was also a 19th century beerhouse, known as the Cherry Tree. It is still standing, beside the inner-relief road that opened in 1968. Behind stands the canning factory situated in the former St Nicholas Works of Charles Burrell & Sons Ltd. [Photograph courtesy of Thetford Town Council]

NORFOLK CANNERIES, MINSTERGATE c.1950

A canning factory was first located on a site close to the Town Bridge in the early 1930s. It employed only about 15 people, before moving to Minstergate in 1946. The Thetford canneries soon expanded and by 1955 over 200 were employed. The canning of fruit and vegetables continued to be an important local industry until production ceased in 1980.

From this photograph it is obvious that automated packaging machinery was still something for the future, at least at Thetford's canneries.

MINSTERGATE, 1984

The canning factory was a mixture of buildings from different periods, from sturdy, brick-built, Victorian structures to more modern, prefabricated structures of less durable materials and generally built after 1946, when Norfolk Canneries first occupied the site. Once the canning factory closed in 1980, the site became a sad and derelict ruin for a few years and then it was demolished for a new supermarket and car park that opened in 1986. One of the few buildings to have survived the 20th century in this part of the town is on the left, the former Paint Shop of Charles Burrell & Sons Ltd that opened as the Charles Burrell Museum in 1991.

MINSTERGATE, 1985

In the first quarter of the 20th century, when this site was occupied by Charles Burrell & Sons and then Agricultural & General Engineers, the sound of a busy engineering works not only reverberated around this area but, at times, could be heard all over the town as boilermakers hammered and shaped the metal. The 20th century witnessed the demise of the steam engine working in the town as more efficient forms of power came to the fore. Perhaps, it is not surprising that much of the former St Nicholas Works has been created into parking space for vehicles powered by the internal combustion engine.

MINSTERGATE, 1986

At one time in the 1960s, when the site for a town centre shopping precinct was being discussed, it was considered this part of the town might be suitable for such a scheme. Eventually, however, it was the industrial area on the east side of the Town Bridge that was chosen. However, retail development became the fate of the site after Keymarket's built and opened this new supermarket in 1986.

ST NICHOLAS STREET, c.1967

Before the railway arrived in 1845 this road lead directly to Mundford. In the first-half of the 19th century this was called Back Street and even though it was renamed St Nicholas Street well before the beginning of the 20th century, it continued to be called 'Back Street' by many locals well into the 1960s. Modern houses were built on the open area, on the right, in the late 1980s. Earlier in the century, flint cottages fronted the street and an old malt house stood immediately behind. [Photograph courtesy of Thetford Town Council]

ST NICHOLAS STREET, c.1965

In 1967 St Nicholas Street was bisected by the construction of the 'inner-relief road'. By then, however, other major changes had already taken place when all sorts of buildings, that had stood in the street for many years, were demolished. Ironically, even at the end of the 20th century, however, several sites in this part of the town had yet to be developed. [Photograph courtesy of Thetford Town Council] **Inset c.1945:** Thetford boasted numerous back street and corner shops in the first six decades of the century. There were several shops in St Nicholas Street, including that of Selwyn 'Sam' Goodley who opened a small shop at his home, number 58 in the 1930s. Goodley's closed in the mid-1960s. [Photograph courtesy of Norah Goodley]

ST NICHOLAS STREET, 1984

In the late 1940s there were over sixty residences in St Nicholas Street, houses, cottages and at least one large house that was divided into apartments or flats. There was also a branch store of the Thetford Co-op, three corner shops, a café and the Rose & Crown pub. It was an interesting mixture of residential, commercial and industrial premises. Many will remember it as a very different street in appearance and character than that at the end of the 20th century.

On the right is one of the few buildings that survived demolition. In the early 1990s it became the sales room of a carpet and flooring company. Nearly opposite is Bidwell Court, a residential, four-storey, block of flats built in 1966, and named after one of Thetford's prominent families of an earlier era.

Less than a decade after this photograph was taken, Breckland District Council's large, office complex, 'Breckland House', was built on the site of the car park. It was officially opened by Queen Elizabeth in 1993.

ST NICHOLAS STREET, c.1966

These former maltings provided accommodation for troops billeted in the town during the 1939-45 War. When photographed, they were the premises of builders merchant Marlow & Co who traded from there until they moved to new premises in Grove Lane, vacated by Precasters Ltd, in 1971. Many of the town's old maltings were demolished at different times during the 20th century and, the few that remain, converted to other uses.

ST NICHOLAS STREET, c.1965

This fine looking house was built by London brewers Whitbread about 1907, on the site of a 19th century brewery and beerhouse owned by Thomas Lusher. The St Nicholas Stores public house became known as 'The London' and was taken over by Moss & Potter of Thetford in 1921. After closure in 1932, soon after the closure of the nearby St Nicholas Works, it became a private residence before demolition in the late 1960s.

WHITE HART STREET

'Bridge Street and White Hart Street, once the main London thoroughfare, slope gently down to the river, lined by good 17th and 18th century buildings.'
Thetford Town Centre Plan 1977 Review Discussion Document, Breckland District Council

WHITE HART STREET, c.1905

Until 1968, White Hart Street formed part of the town's main thoroughfare, the A11 road between Newmarket and Norwich. For motorists, pedestrians and local traders it was often a frequent cause of concern as large motor vehicles negotiated, even if at times very slowly, the narrow commercial street in both directions.

Although the shopkeepers' wares and services have changed during the century, White Hart Street has, generally, escaped the same degree of redevelopment that has touched many other parts of the old town centre.

When photographed, the shop in the foreground, number 1 White Hart Street, was that of fancy draper & gent's outfitter, Thomas Pett, who began trading from there at the end of the 19th century. From the early 1930s until closure in 1974, it was occupied by grocers, Ben & George Palmer. For a few years, until 1999, it served as a Jehovah Witness Kingdom Hall before being converted into the premises of an estate agent.

WHITE HART STREET, c.1960

In 1921, Prince Fredrick Duleep Singh, of Blo' Norton Hall near Thetford, an enthusiastic local historian and collector, purchased numbers 21 and 23 White Hart Street to be converted into a museum for the town. During the internal renovations many fine features of Tudor architecture were discovered, before it opened as The Ancient House Museum in December 1924. The signboard that hangs above the front entrance was given by Norwich brewers Bullard. Perhaps it had previously hung outside one of their public houses.

WHITE HART STREET, c.1910

The shop front on the right is that of confectioner, J.E. Brown. It was known as the Chocolate Box until 1967 when the shop and adjoining houses were demolished for the 'inner relief road'. Just beyond the shop is Grey Gables, for many years the home of the Tyrrell family. The last to live there was Sarah Rebecca Tyrrell, who died there in 1929, the same house in which she was born ninety years earlier. In 1974, Grey Gables opened as the Thomas Paine Hotel.

On the opposite side of the road is Wereham House, then, the ivy-clad home of local merchant, Mr Arthur Cronshey. In 1955 it became the local headquarters of the Royal British Legion and from 1988, a guest house.

WHITE HART STREET, c.1915

In the foreground is Grey Gables, later the Thomas Paine Hotel, while the former Fleece Inn stands at the junction of the Croxton and Norwich Road. The Fleece closed in the 1880s and by the 1920s it was the property of St Cuthbert's Church; the garden was the bowling green of St Cuthbert's Bowling Club. Later, it was known as St Andrew's Way and then a private school run by Mr William Kennedy. The school closed in the mid-1960s and the building was demolished soon afterwards. In 1976 a new office complex was built, on what was once the garden, called 'Crown Offices'. Departments for the Traffic Examiner, Ordnance Survey, and Department of Health and Social Services worked from there for a few years.

Behind the old Fleece Inn can be seen the almshouses erected in Croxton Road by Sarah Rebecca Tyrrell in the 1880s.

KING STREET

'Since the mid-1960s most of King Street's old established businesses and the premises they occupied have been replaced.'. David Osborne, *'Thetford Gleanings',* published 2003

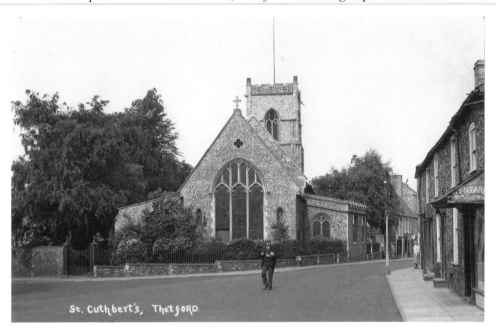

ST CUTHBERT'S CHURCH, c.1925

It is probable that a church or chapel dedicated to Saint Cuthbert has stood on this site since the town was in its infancy, over one thousand years ago. For much of the 20th century, during the pre-overspill period when the town's population was no more than 5,500, there were three ancient Anglican churches in the town holding regular Sunday services. Remarkably, despite the town's considerable population growth, St Cuthbert's is the only ancient church to survive as a place of regular worship.

KING STREET, c.1905

The shop on the right is that of Harry 'Hotty' Webster, just before he sold out to Mr A.J. Savage in 1905. Savage's closed early in 1962 and although it is over forty years since Savage's closed, many old Thetfordians still remember it with some affection. Its general appearance and atmosphere continue to stir fond memories of a lost age, of an era when shopping and many other things were done so differently. Savage's old shop was demolished in 1962 to make way for a new retail development now occupied by Superdrug and Halifax Building Society.

KING STREET, c.1935

Next door to Savage Bros at number 8 was H. Green, printer, stationer and bookseller. Henry Green began trading from there in 1883. The shop was situated, naturally enough, at the front of the premises and among the goods sold by Henry Green were picture postcards of the town and other local souvenirs. In 1916 Green's also advertised a 'repository & circulating library', when there was no public library in Thetford. Green's printing department at the rear of the premises was closed in 1960 and Green's shop in 1984.

KING STREET, c.1910

Captivating scenes such as this, taken in the early 1900s, are now beyond living memory. The shop in the right foreground is number 13, the bicycle and motor cycle shop of J.G. Brown. Besides making his own bicycles, J.G. Brown was also a motor engineer who sold motor spirit [petrol] and oil from his King Street premises. Next door at number 11 was ironmonger, George Brown, the town's Mayor in 1912. Both shops were purchased by local businessman B.C. Culey in 1955 and demolished in 1960 along with the adjoining property, a former nursing home, to make way for the Woolworth's store that opened in 1961. Certainly since the 1960s many of Thetford's locally owned, town centre, retail outlets or shops have disappeared to be replaced by national retailers.

KING STREET, 1902

This photograph captures King Street not only decorated with flags and bunting to celebrate the Coronation of King Edward VII in August 1902 but also a good supply of horse muck. For ladies, in particular, at a time when long dresses were everyday fashion, crossing the road must have been a hazardous journey. After the 1914-18 War, as ladies' dresses became shorter in length, the horse and cart gradually became less common about the town and after the 1939-45 War it was by then a rarity.

KING STREET, c.1926

Although the volume of vehicular traffic was never a real problem in King Street in the 1920s, some people were already complaining about motor vehicles parking and causing an obstruction in King Street, Bridge Street and White Hart Street. On the left is the dairy shop of Robert Rinder. Opposite is the King's Arms public house that closed in 1927. It was sold for £650 the following year and became known as the Ye Olde King's Arms Tea Rooms before demolition in 1936.

KING STREET, c.1910

Besides the King's House there were several large, fashionable and desirable houses in King Street in the early years of the century. Several large houses can be seen in this view. In the right foreground is number 21 and next door on the corner of Tanner Street is number 19, the home of Dr. P.R.J.B. Minns and now the site of Lloyds TSB. On the opposite corner of Tanner Street is number 17, where Thomas R. Pett and his family lived for many years. Mr Pett had a draper's shop in White Hart Street, when most shopkeepers still lived in accommodation above or behind their shops.

KING STREET, 1996

King Street's appearance changed very little in the first five decades of the century but the next fifty years were ones of numerous and radical changes. Many once familiar buildings were demolished as properties changed hands, creating a new and different commercial centre. In 1974 most of the street was created into a pedestrianized precinct and in the mid-1990s the street was resurfaced and generally improved.

KING STREET, c.1935

The building on the right is the former Chequers public house that closed in 1921. In 1935 it was number 42 King Street, the premises of licensed game and poultry dealer, Herbert Ellis. It was a popular shop for all kinds of fish, fruit, game, eggs, poultry, rabbits and block ice. On the opposite side of the street, at number 23, is the shop of jeweller, gold & silver smith, S. Munroe. Next door at 25, was bookseller & newsagent J.W. Clarke.

KING'S HOUSE, c.1955

The King's House was once owned by King James I and there is a tradition that it stands on the site of a much earlier medieval manor house. For the first five decades of the 20th century, the King's House was a private residence for several different people. The last was retired Yorkshire businessman, Mr George W. Staniforth who died there in 1947 and bequeathed the house and its extensive gardens to the town. Five years after the death of G.W. Staniforth, the King's House became the municipal offices and chambers of Thetford Borough Council. [Photograph courtesy of Studio Five, Thetford]

THOMAS PAINE STATUE, 1964

Thetford's first memorial to its most famous son was a plaque set into the base of a street lamp erected in the 1920s, standing at the centre of the junction of Station Road, White Hart Street and Croxton Road. This was followed in 1943 by a plaque, erected by American servicemen, on the exterior of Grey Gables, White Hart Street, close to where Thomas Paine was born in 1737.

The gilded statue of Thomas Paine was unveiled in June 1964, a gift to the town from the Thomas Paine Foundation of America. It was sculptured by the President of the Royal Academy, Sir Charles Wheeler. This photograph captures part of the unveiling ceremony, performed by the Mayor of Thetford, Richard Easten.

KING STREET, 1962

This photograph, taken outside the Bell Hotel, looks across into Minstergate where the entrance to Charlie Pearson's café can be seen. Pearson's café was a popular 'working class' resort especially for those enjoying a break amidst their toil and labour and still clad in their soiled working attire. What better time for a hot mug of tea and a tasty bread roll? Earlier in the century Charlie had a bakery business in St Nicholas Street and later in St Mary's Row. On the corner at number 2 Bridge Street is men's and boy's outfitter B.N. Pett and on the opposite corner is Palmer's Stores. [Photograph courtesy of Thetford Town Council]

WELL STREET and TANNER STREET

'Tanning – the process of converting raw animal hides and skins into leather is probably a very ancient local craft.' David Osborne, *'There's Nothing Like Leather',* Thetford Magazine, No 29, Summer 2007

WELL STREET, 1966

Although new 'overspill' factories and housing estates began to be built on the outskirts of the town in 1958, changes to the old town centre did not really begin until the mid-1960s. One important development in the town centre in the 1960s was the construction of the Carnegie Room an extension to the existing Guildhall. The cottages that stood on the east side of Well Street have already been cleared for the new development. Gradually, the remaining cottages and the attractive row of dwellings on the opposite side of the street became heaps of rubble. One of the last buildings to survive demolition was Allison's sweet and tobacco shop.

ALLISON'S, WELL STREET, c.1965

Confectionery and tobacco was sold from this shop, number 2 Well Street, for many years run by Albert F. Smith in the 1920s, C. Robinson in the 1930s, R. & E. McCaskie in the 1940s then E.C. Brown and finally Clifford and Isobel Allison from the mid-1950s until closure in April 1967, prior to the redevelopment of the west side of Well Street.

In 1971 Allison's old shop was demolished for a new office of the Norwich Building Society that opened in 1973, while St Cuthbert's ancient churchyard was modified to make way for a new development behind Allison's old shop. [Photograph courtesy of Thetford Town Council]

WELL STREET, c.1920

Although there were never many retail shops in Well Street, master basket maker William Frost traded at number 17 from about 1912 until 1927, when he moved his business to Hertfordshire. The premises were later occupied for many years by watchmaker & jeweller, James A. Goodman. [Photograph courtesy of Margaret Vidall]

WELL STREET and TANNER STREET, 1970

The edifice of St Cuthbert's Church looks upon a scene of almost total destruction. A separate development was that of Allison's old shop and a house that stood behind, for many years a dentist's surgery that can still be seen standing. An endearing part of the old town had quickly been swept away, to be replaced with a large store and seven shops with flats above, that generally, were soon considered to be much less appealing and, arguably, of less commercial value than what went before. [Photograph courtesy of Thetford Town Council]

THE OLD HOUSE. THETFORD 84.

TANNER STREET, c.1912

The jettied building in the foreground is the only building still standing at the end of the 20th century. It is now the Old Coach House, a florist's shop. Adjacent can be seen a small house with two window casements and then, 'The Old House', that once belonged to the Cronsheys, a prominent local family in the 19th and early 20th centuries. It was demolished about 1930. Also to be seen is the west gable of the Manor House, a very old house that was demolished in 1967 to make way for the County Library.

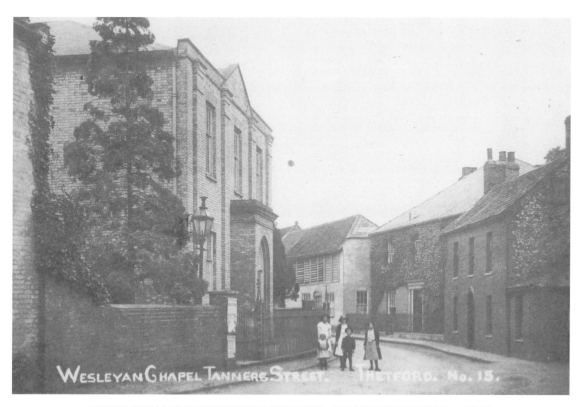

WESLEYAN METHODIST CHAPEL, TANNER TREET, c.1915

The Wesleyan Chapel opened in 1830 and became the Methodist Chapel in the 1930s when the Primitive Methodist and Wesleyan Methodist Church united. The Methodist Chapel might easily have been demolished and relocated when plans were being put forward to redevelop the town centre in the 1960s. Thetford's Methodists, however, dismissed the proposals and agreed to stay and even extend their Tanner Street premises.

METHODIST CHURCH HALL, TANNER STREET, 1961

An old furniture warehouse belonging to Glasswell's of Bury St Edmunds and adjacent to the Tanner Street Methodist Chapel, was acquired by Thetford's Methodists in 1960. It was converted into a Church Hall and opened in 1961. Further extensions were added to the Methodist Church Hall in 1982. For many years the Church Hall has been a popular venue for all sorts of events such as church bazaars, concerts and Saturday coffee mornings, when friends and acquaintances meet to chat over a cup of coffee or tea.

TANNER STREET, 1967

This photograph was taken from King Street, soon after demolition work had begun to create the Riverside Walk shopping precinct that opened in October 1968. The partly demolished building was previously the grocery and general store of C.H. Norman. The site is now occupied by Lloyds TSB. The industrial and residential buildings that stood in Tanner Street, north of the Methodist Chapel, were also demolished to make way for shops and a branch of the Westminster Bank that opened in February, 1969. [Photograph courtesy of Thetford Town Council]

TANNER STREET, 1970

This was the junction of Tanner Street and King Street until 1974 when King Street and this end of Tanner Street were closed to all vehicular traffic and the area pedestrianized. This end of Tanner Street, just beyond the Tan House, then officially became part of the Riverside Walk.

The site of the old tannery is the car park behind Tan House. The Thetford Leather Manufacturing Company ceased trading at the tannery in 1928 and although the business was then taken over by a limited company, it is believed that the tannery became redundant soon afterwards.

BRIDGE STREET and LONDON ROAD

'In view of the importance of the Town Bridge river crossing the approximate alignments London Road-Bridge Street-White Hart Street, and perhaps of Castle Street-King Street-Minstergate are likely to be ancient'. Alan Crosby, *'A History of Thetford',* published 1986

BRIDGE STREET, c.1905

In the early years of the 20th century, Bridge Street was part of the town's main thoroughfare and, as such, one of the town's main commercial streets, lined with a variety of shops, a bank and the Bell Hotel on the corner of King Street. The Bell Corner was then a popular rendezvous for some local men, to stand and 'mardle', and watch the world go by.

In 1919, a woman died after being run over by a motor car at the Bell Corner and by the mid-1920s, with the *'peril of growing motor traffic'*, there were calls for improvements to be made at the Bell Corner junction, such as the painting of white lines on the road surface.

BARCLAYS BANK, BRIDGE STREET, 1997

There has been a bank on this site, at least, since the 1840s, when it was the bank of Harvey & Hudson. By the early years of the 20th century it was the bank of Barclay & Co Ltd, open daily from 10–4 and on Saturdays 10–1. As the town's population increased during the 20th century, so did the services offered at Barclays Bank. Moreover, customers were greeted with a new image when the façade and interior were given a new, modern look in 1964. Barclays was the first bank to introduce a credit card in the UK in 1966 and an Automatic Telling Machine in 1967. An ATM or cash point machine was first introduced at Thetford's branch of Barclays in 1982.

BRIDGE STREET, c.1905

When this photograph was taken, most of the vehicular traffic passing through the narrow Bridge Street was horse-drawn, although there were a few horseless carriages powered by the internal combustion engine and, of course, steam-powered traction engines, many of them manufactured in the town. The children standing beside the Town Bridge, posing for the photographer, probably lived to see, not only long queues of motor traffic as it slowly made its way through the town, but also the demolition of many old buildings to make way for parking space for the motor car. Bridge Street continued to form part of the main road through the town until 1968, when the 'inner relief road' was opened.

THE ANCHOR HOTEL, 1965

Like the Bell Hotel, standing close by, from the very early years of the 20th century, the Anchor Hotel was ideally situated to cater for the increasing number of passing motorists. As the number of motorists increased, along with the growth of the town, both hotels expanded, increasing the number of beds and other facilities. This photograph captures painters at work putting the finishing touches to the facade after a large extension was completed on the south side of the old hotel while allowing vehicle access to the essential car park.

LONDON ROAD, c.1905

This photograph, taken from the tower of St Mary's Church, shows the London Road and several other parts of the town in the early years of the 20th century. In the centre foreground is the rear of the Girls' Grammar School and to the right is a large house, built in the early 1880s for the Headmaster of the Boys' Grammar School and 20 boarders. Opposite is the Boys' Grammar School and beyond, in the centre of the view, can be seen the chimney of the St Nicholas Works that was demolished in 1960. Further to the right is the chimney of Thetford's electricity generating station, standing between St Nicholas Street and White Hart Street. In the far distance can be seen a group of maltings that once stood close to the railway station.

LONDON ROAD, c.1915

The building in the right foreground is the Capital & Counties Bank Ltd, before it was acquired by Lloyds Bank Ltd in 1918. The Lloyds Bank continued trading from London Road until 1968, when a new, purpose-built bank was opened on the corner of King Street and Tanner Street.

The large house on the right, just before the row of lime trees, is aptly named The Limes. In the distance is the Presbytery of St Mary's Roman Catholic Church.

ST MARY'S CATHOLIC CHURCH, LONDON ROAD, c.1905

When Thetford's Catholic Church was built on the edge of the town in 1826, it was the first Catholic church to be built in the town since before the Reformation. The church building was far less remote once the Newtown Estate was built to the south in the 1920s. The Presbytery or priest's house stands on the left and, adjacent, is the church with the single-storey entrance porch. Hidden behind the church, at the rear, is a small Church Hall that was originally built as a school in the late 1870s and paid for by Mrs Lyne Stephens of Lynford Hall, near Mundford. The Catholic School was maintained by the Thetford School Board but closed in 1903. In more recent times, the Church Hall has frequently been used as a Polling Station for local and national government elections.

NEWTOWN, 1929

During the 1914-18 Great War, at least two hutted army camps were built south of the town just off the London Road. One of these stood adjacent to St Mary's Catholic Church. Soon after the war the camp was closed and in 1920 the huts sold off at a public auction held on the site. The 9 acres [3.6 hectares] of land was purchased by Thetford Borough Council for the Newtown Estate that was completed by 1926.

In 1974, Thetford Borough Council's housing stock was handed over to the newly formed Breckland District Council. Following the Housing Act 1980 and the introduction of the Right to Buy Scheme, many of the BDC's sitting tenants began the process of buying their homes.

LONDON ROAD, c.1960

The Thetford Town Sign was a gift from Thetford Chamber of Commerce and accepted on behalf of the town by the Mayor, Mrs Sybil Wheeler, in October 1954.

Until Thetford Borough Council built Fulmerston Road, Icknield Way and Icknield Close between the late 1940s and mid-1950s, the Newtown Estate was on the extreme periphery of the town. By the time that this photograph was taken, the 'Overspill' had begun and many more houses had been built or were planned on the agricultural land between the Bury Road and London Road.

LONDON ROAD, 1971 & 1988

Until the early 1960s, apart from the Cemetery, most of the land either side of the London Road, south of the Icknield Way junction, was Borough Council allotments, arable fields and pasture. Soon after the 'overspill' development began, this land was rapidly transformed into new housing and industrial estates. For people living and working on these new estates, crossing the busy A11 London Road was often a hazardous affair and, inevitably, pedestrians were involved in one or two fatal accidents. It was following the death of a young girl, near the Norfolk Plover public house in 1970, that mothers along with their children from the neighbouring area protested. They blocked the road on several occasions and also petitioned for a pedestrian crossing to be built. The following year, after much consultation, Norfolk County Council agreed to erect a large, steel, footbridge over the busy road at a reported cost of £12,000. [Photograph 1971 courtesy of Archant]

THETFORD CAMP, c.1919

Besides the army camp near St Mary's Catholic Church, a much larger camp, known as Thetford Camp, was erected in 1916, on land further to the south of the town close to the London Road. This area is now part of the Thetford Forest, just south of the Burrell Way industrial estate. During the 1914-18 Great War, thousands of troops passed through Thetford Camp and, once the conflict ended, it then became a large demobilization centre. Thetford Camp finally closed in 1921 and the huts were soon dismantled and disposed of at a public auction held on the site.

This is the YMCA where troops could 'pass an hour", relaxing, reading, writing letters home, playing billiards or enjoying some light refreshments. During the war the Guildhall also served as a temporary YMCA for the troops billeted in and around the town.

THE LITTLE OUSE RIVER

'The Little or Lesser Ouse has its source in the Lopham Fen, 10 miles east of Thetford.'
David Osborne, *'A Portrait of Thetford Brandon & District in Old Picture Postcards'*, published 1990

TOWN BRIDGE, c.1965

The town of Thetford owes its existence to the two rivers now called the Little Ouse and the Thet, that slowly flow through the town. It is probable that people have been crossing the river, where the Town Bridge stands, from the earliest times. The Town Bridge was built in the 19th century for the carriage of horses and carts but continued to serve the 20th century traveller, frequently carrying very heavy motor vehicles, something it was not designed for.

During the 1960s when there was much redevelopment taking place in the Bridge Street area, the Town Bridge was closed, for a few weeks, to all traffic. A temporary footbridge was erected while the work was in progress. [Photograph courtesy of Thetford Town Council]

TOWN BRIDGE & LITTLE OUSE RIVER, 1996

The Town Bridge ceased carrying heavy volumes of motor traffic once the 'inner relief' road was opened in 1968. Although there were numerous changes to the area around this important river crossing during the 20th century, the cast-iron Town Bridge survived the upheaval, even though its appearance was transformed with a new, multi-colour paint scheme in the 1980s.

THE LITTLE OUSE, 1912

The local rivers flooded many times during the 20th century. This photograph captures the river viewed from the Town Bridge, towards the Haling Path, during the severe floods that struck Norfolk, after several hours of torrential rain, in August 1912. Although the local rivers burst their banks and there was some localized flooding, unlike some places in Norfolk, there was little structural damage or loss of life.

THE LITTLE OUSE, 1984

On the left is the former canning factory that operated from this site, beside the river, from 1946 until closure in 1980. The site was previously occupied by Charles Burrell & Sons Ltd who manufactured a variety of steam-powered traction engines and agricultural machines until closure in the late 1920s.

After the canning factory closed the site became derelict for a few years and, soon after this photograph was taken, it was demolished to make way for a supermarket and car park that opened in 1986.

LITTLE OUSE and HALING PATH, c.1910

Until 1930, when the Great Ouse Catchment Board was formed, the Corporation of Thetford was responsible for the general maintenance of the Little Ouse, a navigable river in the early years of the century. In the 1980s the National Rivers Authority took on this responsibility followed by the Environment Agency in the mid-1990s.

The boat in the picture is probably the one used by the Corporation, for the annual weed cutting operation. On other occasions, parts of the river were also dredged to remove silt.

RIVERSIDE WALK and LITTLE OUSE RIVER, 1968

Several large, malting houses occupied this part of the town, beside the Little Ouse, until the mid-1960s. Eventually, they were sold and demolished to make way for the town's first shopping precinct, the Riverside Walk, officially opened by the Mayor in October 1968. [Photograph courtesy of Thetford Town Council]

RIVERSIDE CAR PARK and COACH STATION, 1995

The Riverside car park was also opened in 1968, the same year that Butten Bridge was erected, connecting the car park to Butten Island and the Riverside Walk. The award winning bridge was constructed by Boulton & Paul of Norwich. It is at this point, under Butten Bridge that the rivers Little Ouse and Thet meet.

In January 1974 Thetford's bus and coach station was opened in the area immediately behind the Anchor Hotel. A well known feature in the car park, from the early 1990s, is the mobile kiosk from where hot drinks and food are sold.

THE LITTLE OUSE and TOWN BRIDGE, 1996

Since the creation of the Riverside Walk and car park, on the opposite side of the river, in the late 1960s, this part of the river has become much more accessible and a welcome attraction to both locals and visitors. Moreover, this part of the river has proved a popular and successful habitat for ducks, geese, moorhens and swans.

THE PULP WORKS, 1975

By the beginning of the 20th century, it is likely that there had been some form of industrial activity on this site, continuously, for about 1,000 years. Pulp ware was first made here in the last quarter of the 19th century and, though still affectionately known as the Pulp Works in the 1970s, the production of pulp ware had been replaced for many years by new processes and materials.

Thetford Moulded Products sold the site for residential development and moved to a new factory on the Fison Way Industrial Estate in 1989.

SPRING MEADOW, THETFORD

THE SPRING MEADOW and WALK, c.1910

Cattle, goats and horses could still be found grazing in several parts of the town in the early years of the 20th century, including on the Spring Meadow beside the Little Ouse.

The Spring Walk has been a popular promenade for Thetfordians and visitors to the town since it was created in the first quarter of the 19th century. However, it was only officially presented to the town in 1940, a gift from Miss Georgina Bidwell and her sister.

THE LITTLE OUSE, 1997

Even for those who remember once bathing and swimming here, it is difficult to imagine that this was the Corporation Swimming Bath, situated for 50 yards [46 metres] along the banks of the Little Ouse. All that has survived is the concrete bank that was constructed in 1922, where diving boards and about two dozen bathing sheds once stood. The changing sheds or cubicles were no more than a long row of crude, wooden, creosoted huts. Besides the individual changing cubicles, there was also a large communal one for males and one for females. At the west end, at the entrance, was a small hut for the pool attendant. The pool had closed by 1971 when an indoor pool was opened on the Croxton Road.

AROUND the MILL HEAD and RIVER THET

'A forgotten amenity, an overlooked beauty. That, say many Thetford people, is the river in the town.'
Thetford & Watton Times, 12 August 1960

THE WATER MILL and MILL HEAD, c1935

Although the Water Mill and the area around the Mill Head were once the centre of much industrial activity, even into the 1960s, the river and riverside close to the Mill Head still retained a beauty and charm of its own. So much so, it featured on numerous photographs, some of which were published on picture postcards and sent to many parts of the country and abroad. Artists have also endeavoured to capture something of its picturesqueness on canvas.

The flags decorating the exterior of the mill are, most probably, to celebrate the Silver Jubilee of King George V.

THE MILL HEAD, 2000

Since the early 1960s, the area around the Mill Head has seen numerous, 'piecemeal' changes, certainly since some of the old industrial buildings close to the river side began to disappear. Later, the area where a small, timber yard stood was landscaped in the mid-1980s and further improved and given a much deserved face-lift in 1989. This included the construction of a small refreshment kiosk, adorned with an old fashioned weather-cock. During the summer months, the kiosk is a very popular rendezvous for locals and visitors to sit and relax, beside the peaceful waters of the River Thet, yet so close to the town centre.

THE WATER MILL, c.1910

Besides several wind mills, centuries ago there were also a number of water mills in the Borough of Thetford. By the early years of the 20th century, however, there were no wind mills and only two water mills remained. One of these was the mill that straddles the River Thet, and anciently known as the Pitt Mill. In the early years of the 20th century, it changed ownership several times. Firstly, in 1906, Josiah Vavasseur of Kilverstone Hall purchased it for £2,000 from Lady Maud Buxton. Then, in 1913, it was sold to Mr George Keymer, who leased the mill to J. Mayes who had previously held it. The mill was last used for grinding grain in the mid-1920s and, in the 1930s, became the premises of the Ibex Coffee Co Ltd for processing and packing tea and coffee. Some locals still call it the 'Coffee Mill', although its industrial life ceased in 1956. Since the early 1960s it has been a Masonic Hall.

THE WATER MILL, 1975

When Thetford's 'overspill' development began in the late 1950s, the single-storey building in the centre and adjacent buildings were used as temporary factories, for a small number of businesses, while they waited for their factories to be completed on the new industrial estates. Not long after this photograph was taken, these buildings were demolished as the town's industrial scene continued to change.

Throughout the 20th century, this area of the town was prone to flooding, most notably in 1912, 1939, 1947, 1968 and 1987.

ST JOHN HALL, NETHER ROW, 1994

The St John Hall was originally built as a chapel for Thetford's Wesleyan Methodists in the very early years of the 19th century. In the first half of the 20th century it was used as a classroom and woodwork room for pupils from the Norwich Road School. When offered for sale in 1952 it was known as the Gospel Hall and soon afterwards, it opened as the St John Hall for the Thetford St John Ambulance Brigade.

SCHOOL LANE, c.1965

The high, flint and chalk wall, marks the boundary of the garden of the White Horse Inn that closed in 1927 then becoming a private house and later a guest house known as the White House.

In the early 1980s, the upper part of the flint and brick wall was demolished and a doctors' surgery was built on the land immediately behind.

BLACKBURN'S YARD from SCHOOL LANE, c.1965

The assortment of buildings and property that stood beyond the closed, wooden gates was known in the 1930s as Blackburn's Yard from where W. Blackburn & Co traded as coal merchants. The little piece of road in front of the yard was then known as Water Mill Lane. The building on the right was opened as Thetford Library in 1930. It closed in 1952 when a new library was opened in the former Mechanics Institute and later opened as the premises of turf accountant, Ernie Ketteringham, once off-course betting was legalised in 1960. The cottages and gardens that once stood in School Lane have already disappeared, having been replaced by a few private garages and car parking space. Not long afterwards, in the early 1970s, Blackburn's Yard suffered the same fate when it was turned into a car park.

THE WOOD YARD, MILL HEAD, c.1970

The early history of this site, standing beside the river Thet, including that in the early years of the 20th century, remains shrouded in mystery. However, from about the late 1930s, it was Vic Dann's woodyard where timber was cut into small logs for delivery to the many houses in the town that used coal and wood to heat the home. This was, of course, in the days before gas or oil-fired central heating became common. Vic's yard became obsolete in the early 1980s and in 1987 the site was cleared and landscaped.

AROUND THE MILLHEAD, c.1960

This interesting aerial view clearly illustrates the assortment of buildings that once stood close to the Mill Head. Vic Dann's wood yard can be seen in the left foreground, beside the River Thet. The Water Mill straddles the river Thet and, adjacent, is the old Mill House that has since been renamed 'Coffee House'. In the centre stand four industrial buildings that were previously used by the coffee processing and packaging company that occupied the Water Mill from 1936 to 1956. Cottages and gardens stand on the south side of the narrow School Lane. St John Hall stands on the corner of School Lane and Nether Row. Standing in the top right corner of the photograph is 'Shrublands', the home for many years of Charles Burrell, Jnr [1847-1929] and then from the mid-1930s, that of local businessman and cinema proprietor, Ben Culey. From the 1980s it has been the home of another local businessman, Keith Eldred who renamed the house, 'Riversmeet'. [Photograph courtesy of Thetford Town Council]

THE BRANDON and BURY ROADS

'On the south bank Brandon Road, London Road, Star Lane and Bury Road more or less focus upon the bridge and are presumably Saxon in origin.' Alan Crosby, *'A History of Thetford',* published 1986

THETFORD GOLF LINKS and BRANDON ROAD, c.1920 & c.1930

In the very early years of the 20th century, a large part of the landscape immediately west of the town was water-meadow and arable land but beyond this was a large expanse of heathland, once known as the Great Warren and the habitat for many thousands of rabbits. A part of this ancient landscape, west of the town and either side of the Brandon Road, was made into a golf course or links soon after a Thetford Golf Club was formed in June 1912. About the same time, a club house was built close to the 18th hole, north of the Brandon Road.

BRANDON ROAD, 1985

By the time that this photograph was taken, from the roof of a house appropriately called 'Warren Edge', the local rabbit population had declined drastically and much of the landscape in this view formed Thetford golf course. The number 1 tee can be seen in the foreground. However, it is a scene that was completely transformed before the end of the 20th century. The Thetford Bypass, that opened in 1989, was routed through what is the middle distance of this view. A motel called 'The Warrener', now stands on the land in the foreground. Moreover, on the opposite side of the Brandon Road is Coney Close, a residential estate built in the 1990s and yet another name linking the area to former days, when rabbits or 'coneys' were farmed on the Great Warren.

BRANDON ROAD, 1965

Between 1948-1959 professional archaeologists excavated, for the first time, several large areas of the town south of the river. While much was discovered about Thetford's ancient past, there were many more questions that needed to be answered. During the summers of 1964-66, archaeologists continued their work just south of the Brandon Road, an area that had been agricultural land for centuries but was now scheduled for development as part of the town's 'overspill' scheme. Archaeological excavations continued once again in 1988-89, piecing together the early history and development of Thetford, once an important Saxon town.

From the many exciting and interesting archaeological discoveries made around the Brandon Road and Red Castle Furze, it is clearly a landscape rich in the evidence of past settlement, even before the town of Thetford existed. In the area close to the present Brandon Road, people were living and carrying out many human activities as early as the first century AD and during many later periods. Also excavated and revealed during the 20th century, were the remains of the Town Ditch and the Red Castle, an 11th century ring-ditch fortification. What is now the Brandon Road may well have been a feature as early as the 9th–10th centuries.

THE PRIORY of the HOLY SEPULCHRE, BRANDON ROAD, 1987

The ruined nave of the priory church of the Canons of the Holy Sepulchre, founded in the 12th century, is another reminder of Thetford's ancient past standing beside the Brandon Road. It is the only surviving priory in England of this small, independent order of Canons. Extensive excavations were carried out here in 1969, prior to a housing development on part of the site.

In the early years of the 20th century, an old farmhouse known as 'The Canons' stood near the ruined church. It formed part of the Croxton Estate and was sold in lots at a public auction in 1934.

BRANDON ROAD, 1988 [top]

The eighteenth green of the old golf course has disappeared under a huge mound of sand, stock-piled for the construction of the A11 Thetford Bypass. A few years after the sand was removed and the bypass opened, a small residential estate known as Coney Close was built on the site.

The main contractors, May Gurney, began constructing the bypass in April 1988 and a part single, part dual carriageway was opened in November the following year. In 1990 a second carriageway was opened.

BURY ROAD, 1987

This part of the Bury Road once formed the east end of the Brandon Road, before changes created in 1967-68 for the new 'inner relief' road.

Since the early 1930s, the open space on the right has been a car park and, at times, an overnight parking area for heavy goods vehicles [HGV's].

In the background is the garage of Ray Powell, formerly, T.H. Nice, and Hanbury & Co.

ST MARY'S ROAD from the BURY ROAD, 1968

This photograph captures the disappearance of St Mary's Road as it is made into a new section of the Bury Road, connecting with the A11 'inner relief' road and the B1107 Brandon Road, at a new junction controlled by traffic lights.

The wall in the left foreground is the north-east corner of St Mary's Churchyard that was demolished for the new road that bisects the once sacred burial ground. [Photograph courtesy of Thetford Town Council]

THE STAR, BURY ROAD, c.1920

Although the Star public house was a popular 'local', nonetheless, it was closed by brewers, Watney Mann [East Anglia] Ltd in January 1970. Soon after closure it was converted into two dwellings.

The Star pub continues to be commemorated by Star Lane that connects Old Bury Road with the newest section of the Bury Road. In the very early years of the 20th century, a blacksmith's shop stood adjacent to the Star, where a small garden is today, at the junction with Star Lane.

BURY ROAD DRIFT, c.1965

Opposite the Old Bury Road junction with Star Lane, is the drift or track that leads off from the Old Bury Road down to the Little Ouse river. It is now a tarmacked access road for the Court House and car park that opened in 1974. The Court House now occupies the area on the right side of the photograph. The only building still standing is the old barn and later garage, in the left foreground, that has been converted into three mews type dwellings. [Photograph courtesy of Thetford Town Council]

BURY ROAD, c.1905

The brick-built houses in the foreground had only just been constructed when this photograph was taken, in the very early years of the 20th century. They were erected on what was then the very outskirts of the town. Only the Gas Works and the Thetford Union Workhouse stood beyond. Opposite was the hedge-lined Grammar School playing field where Thetford's first council houses were built between 1912-14. They were originally known as the Corporation Dwellings but since 1949 they have been known as St Mary's Crescent.

THE GAS WORKS, BURY ROAD, 1951

Although few people in the town owned a motor vehicle in the early 1950s, many more families owned a hand-cart or wheel barrow of some description. These were used for transporting all sorts of goods about the town, such as small items of furniture and other household goods, fuel for the household fire and waste food or swill for pigs and chickens kept in back gardens, on allotments or small holdings scattered about the town.

In the winter months, in particular, there was a steady stream of customers arriving at the Gas Works with empty barrows and hand-carts to collect sacks of coke for the domestic fire. Large quantities of coke, a by-product in the manufacture of gas, were produced at the Gas Works. Even though it had to be collected rather than be delivered, coke was a much cheaper fuel than coal. [Photograph courtesy of Archant]

BARNHAM CROSS COMMON, BURY ROAD, 1948

Messengers on horseback and then horse-drawn coaches carried the Royal Mail to the town in the 18th and early years of the 19th century. Then it was the turn of the railway and, much later, motor vans and other motor vehicles. So it was an interesting novelty when the Royal Mail introduced an experimental helicopter mail service from Peterborough to Great Yarmouth via Thetford in June, 1948. The Sikorski S.51 helicopter belonging to British European Airways and bearing the 'Royal Mail' pennant, also called at seven other towns besides Thetford. When the first flight landed on Barnham Common it was greeted by a large crowd of local people including the Mayor, Councillor H. J. Leach, Thetford's Postmaster, Mr A.F. Cornell and children from local schools. The experiment, however, did not develop into a regular service. [Photograph courtesy of Archant]

ST BARNABAS HOSPITAL, c.1973

The Thetford Union Workhouse or 'Spike', as it was known locally, was built on the extreme outskirts of the town, just off the Bury Road, in the first-half of the 19th century. It was still a workhouse for the first three decades of the 20th century. However, by the early 1950s, when Thetford Borough Council built many more new houses south of the existing town and west of the Bury Road, the old workhouse was known as St Barnabas Hospital for the aged infirm. Even so, many rooms of the large, Victorian buildings remained unoccupied or were simply used as store rooms. In 1970, St Barnabas was closed and four years later work began demolishing the former institution once synonymous with poverty and destitution.

BURY ROAD, 2000

In January 1965, when Murco Petroleum Ltd first built a petrol station on this site, their petrol was retailed at between 4/11½d [25p] and 5/7d [28p] a gallon, depending on the grade. They also offered Green Shield trading stamps as an incentive to customers.

Certainly during the last few decades of the 20th century, so-called 'panic buying' was occasionally prevalent in the town as the supply or availability of various commodities such as bread, sugar and petrol were threatened or perceived to be in short supply. Even in 1973, many years after wartime rationing had ceased, petrol coupons were once again distributed nationally in the expectation of a severe petrol shortage. This photograph captures motorists queuing to fill their vehicles after petrol supplies were once again threatened.

THE NUNNERY

'Not far from the Workhouse is the Benedictine Nunnery of St George. It is said to have been founded by the Abbot of Bury in 1020 in commemoration of the sanguinary conflict between King Edmund and the Danes.'
W.G. Clarke, *'Guide to the Borough of Thetford'*, published 1923

NUNNERY PLACE, c.1910

The 18th century Nunnery Place stands amongst the remains of an ancient Benedictine nunnery that was dissolved in the 16th century and then soon became a private residence known as The Place. Queen Elizabeth I dined there in 1578. For much of the 20th century, the Nunnery estate was a working farm and shooting estate although in the 1920s and 30s it was occupied by Marcel Varipati, a Greek corn merchant, who not only trained racehorses but also established a successful stud for thoroughbred racehorses at the Nunnery, in what was once the nuns' 12th century church dedicated to St George.

In 1990, Patrick and Wendy Rudrum and Jeremy and Carmel Lowndes, between them, gave the Nunnery House, the adjoining former monastic buildings and some 160 acres [65 hectares] of adjoining land to the British Trust for Ornithology [BTO]. The following year it was opened as the BTO's headquarters.

NIGHTINGALE WAY, NUNNERY FIELDS, 1996

The land and property donated to the BTO was part of a business agreement that permitted the Nunnery estate to be developed as a private, residential development – Nunnery Fields. Construction work began in the mid-1990s and the estate's roads were appropriately named after British birds.

THE NUNNERY ARCH, 1986

The brick arch is believed to have been built in the 16th century, perhaps, as a grand entrance to The Place for the visit of Queen Elizabeth in 1578. In 1913, when the boundary wall was repaired, the lower space through the arch was bricked up and the date '1913' inserted into the brickwork. In more recent times this brickwork was removed when the historic archway was renovated.

The houses standing behind form Nunnery Drive, a private residential estate that began to be built in the early 1970s.

THE NUNNERY STUD, 1990

Annual horse races were held in Thetford, probably across part of Barnham Cross Common, in the 18th century. At that time, the Duke of Grafton, of nearby Euston Hall, was amongst the top breeders of thoroughbred racehorses. Many of today's thoroughbreds can trace their lineage back to the Duke's Euston stud.

Although Marcel Varipati bred and trained racehorses at the Nunnery, there were no equine races in the town during the 20th century, apart from the occasional Donkey Derby on the Recreation Ground. Nonetheless, for many locals, the 'Sport of Kings' continued to be a popular attraction, even in the first six decades of the 20th century, before off-course betting shops or 'bookies' were legalized in 1960. Nonetheless, during this period of austerity, there were several men in the town who acted illegally as turf accountants and 'bookies runners', allowing local punters the pleasure of a 'flutter' on horse races held up and down the country.

Since 1961, there have been numerous licensed turf accountants trading in the town. Moreover, the world of top class horse racing has been brought closer to the town, since the Nunnery Stud was built on land that was once part of the large Shadwell Estate in 1987. The Nunnery Stud is an important element in the international, racehorse empire owned by one of the world's top thoroughbred breeders, Sheikh Hamdan bin Rashid Al Maktoum, Deputy Ruler of Dubai. When first opened there was just one stallion at the Nunnery Stud, Green Dessert. This photograph is of an equally famous stallion, Nashwan.

THETFORD OVERSPILL TOWN

'Following the publication last week of the reports of Thetford's "overspill" plans, there was considerable talk in the town about the project and a predominance, as far as could be judged, of enthusiasm for it.'
Thetford & Watton Times, 29 January 1954

THETFORD FROM THE AIR, c.1960

During the 1920s, Thetford's economic and industrial prosperity declined as several of the town's old and once important industries closed; brewing, corn milling, tanning and a relatively new industry that, during the previous century, had developed into the town's largest employer, the St Nicholas Works of Charles Burrell & Sons Ltd where agricultural machinery and steam engines were manufactured. Although Thetford Borough Council and the local Chamber of Commerce were successful in attracting a small number of new industries to the town during the 1930s and 40s, this had little real impact on Thetford's general economic conditions.

Immediately after the 1939-45 War, Thetford's problems seemed trivial compared to many British cities. During the War, thousands of London's houses were destroyed or badly damaged as a result of bombing and, moreover, much that survived was old and poorly maintained. There was a massive shortage of adequate housing for the capital's population. The post-war Government immediately introduced important legislation to help solve London's housing problems - the New Towns Act, 1946. Eight new towns were originally planned within a 30 mile radius of London and four in other parts of the country. Stevenage was the first New Town. In addition to the New Towns Act 1946, the Town Development Act 1952, enabled congested cities and towns to negotiate 'overspill' agreements with existing towns that desired to develop and expand by accepting 'overspill' population from congested areas.

In the early 1950s, Thetford Borough Council was still seeking solutions to the town's employment and economic problems. There was increasing concern that with no major industries, apart from a canning factory and a pulpware manufacturer, the town's long term economic and industrial future appeared bleak, even though, nationally, there was a new optimism. In May, 1952, Peter Baker, MP for South Norfolk, suggested that Thetford Chamber of Trade put forward a plan to attract new industries. It was a view shared by Thetford's new Mayor, John Wilson. Then, in April 1953, it was reported on the front page of the Thetford & Watton Times that Thetford Borough Council and London County Council were proposing to adopt a scheme whereby the town of Thetford become a London 'overspill' town. An agreement was reached in 1955 and Thetford officially became a London 'Overspill' town when Thetford Borough Council, under the Town Development Act 1952, signed a formal agreement with the LCC. It was initially planned that 5,000 Londoners would move to the town. The 'overspill' scheme offered the town hope and a far more prosperous future. Between 1946 and 1970, a total of 21 New Towns were created besides many more 'Overspill' or 'Expanding' Towns.

This fascinating aerial photograph captures the town centre just a few years prior to redevelopment. The Guildhall stands just left of centre. [Photograph courtesy of Thetford Town Council]

BRIDGE STREET, c.1963

Once the 'overspill' work began, there was certainly plenty for Thetfordians to observe and talk about from day to day. While new housing and industrial estates were built on the southern outskirts of the town, many parts of the old town centre that had not really been disturbed for many decades, gradually began to reverberate to the sound of machinery as demolition workers removed the old to make way for the new. Moreover, amongst this activity, Thetford's roads and pavements were frequently disturbed for the laying of additional electric, gas, sewage, telephone and water services for a new town and a rapidly growing population. [Photograph courtesy of Thetford Town Council]

KING STREET, 1962

Soon after the arrival of the first 'overspill' families into their new homes on the outskirts of the town, piecemeal commercial developments began in the town centre. All sorts of old and familiar buildings were demolished, to make way for new shops and offices and the modern architecture they embraced.

The former Chequers public house, that had stood for several centuries adjacent to the Kings House, was demolished and the site cleared for a new W.J. Adkins of Cambridge supermarket. Adkins reign in Thetford ended in 1969, blaming their closure on 'too much competition'.

The former manse of the Baptist Church also succumbed to the same fate as the old Chequers, undergoing demolition for another new retail development in the town's principle high street. [Photographs courtesy of Thetford Town Council]

SWEYN CLOSE, c.1965

The first London County Council [LCC] housing contract, for twenty-five houses, was awarded to local builder, Goddards [1954] Ltd. The contract was soon extended for the construction of a further twenty-one houses. The first new houses were built on an extended Fulmerston Road and Staniforth Road. Once completed they were handed over to Thetford Borough Council and in April 1959, families began arriving from London. That same month, the Rural Dean of Thetford, the Reverend E.C. Brooks, conducted a special service at number 58 Fulmerston Road to bless the *'overspill estate'*. By July 1959, thirty-five families had moved from London into their new Thetford homes. [Photograph courtesy of John Ayton]

KIMMS BELT & PINE CLOSE, c.1965

Families began moving into the brick-built Kimms Belt houses in 1960, but it was two years later before Kimms Belt was finally completed. The new houses were built adjacent to a 'belt' of beech trees that provided a natural barrier between the new housing estate and Thetford's first 'overspill' industrial estate. The Kimm family were 19th century millers and farmers, who occupied a farmhouse that stood close to the London Road, where the Norfolk Plover public house and restaurant was built and opened in 1966. An old tower windmill once stood close by.

In March 1947 there were 144 council houses in the Borough of Thetford; by January 1966 this had increased to nearly 600.

The Pine Close shops were opened in 1962. [Photographs courtesy of John Ayton]

GEORGE WILLIAMS ENGINEERING, c.1960

George Williams Engineering moved from Willesden, north London, to Thetford in 1959. It was the first firm to move from London to Thetford under the 'overspill' agreement and Williams' employees and their families were amongst the first to arrive in the town. The new modern factory, the likes of which had never been seen in the town before, was considered as something of a 'flagship' for this far-reaching enterprise, the 'Thetford overspill' or, as some preferred to call it, Thetford Town Development.

It was a shock to the town and the 120 employees when George Williams Engineering went into receivership in 1963. Soon afterwards, however, the company was taken over by refrigeration engineers Clark-Built Ltd. A new company was formed, Clarke-Built [Williams] Ltd, which traded from Stephenson Way.

Williams former factory premises, leased by Thetford Borough Council, were soon occupied by Hobal Engineering Ltd, manufacturers of stainless steel plant. They had moved to Thetford from London in 1962, initially occupying 4 unit factories on the industrial estate. [Photographs courtesy of John Ayton]

NOVOBORD, c.1965

In July 1961 the Thetford & Watton Times announced, *"Thetford Chosen for New £1¼m Factory"*. Novobord [UK] Ltd of Ealing, London, had chosen a thirty-three acre site [13 hectares] at Thetford for their new factory, producing wood particle board. The construction of the Novobord [UK] Ltd plant or factory began in 1962 and, in October the following year, the factory was officially opened by Sir Geoffrey Ripon, MP. At the time it was the largest factory to have been built and it was envisaged that up to 250 people would be employed at the plant when in full production. Within two years of opening the factory was taken over by Airscrew-Weyroc Ltd. The plant was then closed in October 1965, for nearly two years, after an explosion killed an employee working on the site. Production finally ceased in 1980.

By the end of the century, the former Novobord site was hardly recognizable from that of forty years earlier. Forming part of Burrell Way, the site was occupied by a variety of distribution, manufacturing and retail businesses, besides a large refuse disposal and recycling centre. The weighbridge in the foreground, however, continues to be maintained and operated.

STEPHENSON WAY INDUSTRIAL ESTATE, c.1975 & THE MILL FARM, c.1950

In 1957, the land that was to become the first 'overspill' industrial estate was mostly pasture, part of the 230 acre [93 hectare] Mill Farm, owned by the Crown Estates. The last tenant of the farm was Mr P. Kent-Woolsey and the farmhouse stood where the Norfolk Plover public house was built in 1966.

The first factories to be built were those closest to Kimms Belt, seen just beyond the middle distance in the photograph. Besides George Williams Engineering, other firms to arrive from London in the late 1950s and early 60s included A. & F. Parkes & Co, Caligraving, Edgar J. Saxon Ltd, Electrical Thermometer Ltd, Flexible Drive & Tool Co Ltd, Morley Electrical Services, Raynham Developments Ltd and R.E. Moore & Co. Development of the new industrial estate was initially a slow, gradual process. By July 1961, two years after the first factory began production, there were still only twenty firms or new factories trading on the estate. In 1963 furniture maker Conran & Co opened the largest factory on the estate. It was reported to be the most modern furniture factory in Europe. That same year UCC Filters moved to Thetford, bringing 15 employees with them. By 1966 there were two industrial estates and nearly fifty new firms. By then, however, a few 'overspill' firms had ceased trading for various reasons while others had already expanded considerably and increased production. [Photographs courtesy of Thetford Town Council and Hilda Kent-Woolsey]

BAXTER LABORATORIES LTD, CAXTON WAY INDUSTRIAL ESTATE, c.1964

Development of the Caxton Way Industrial Estate, on the west side of the London Road, began in the early 1960s. Some of the town's largest factories and employers, Baxter Laboratories, Danepak and Thermos were among the first national and international companies to locate to Caxton Way.

American company Baxter Laboratories, began production at their new Thetford factory in November 1965. By 1969 about 250 people were employed at Thetford, producing and supplying various health services with a range of products for people with life threatening conditions. Once companies such as Baxter Laboratories and Danepak began full production, the demand for female workers soon outstripped availability. The situation was further exacerbated once Jeyes factory was in full production in 1970. Even in 1974, it was reported that some local firms were not expanding because of a general labour shortage. [Photograph courtesy of Baxter Healthcare Ltd]

CAXTON WAY INDUSTRIAL ESTATE, c.1970

By the time that this photograph was taken, Baxter Laboratories had already expanded their premises at Thetford. By 1975 Baxters were the largest employer in the town with over one thousand employees. When this photograph was taken, work was soon to start on the construction of a large office block and factory for air distribution equipment manufacturer, Trox Brothers of Enfield, London. Their new Thetford premises were completed in October, 1971, initially employing about 135.

Ever since Thetford's industrial estates began to be built and developed in the late 1950s, it has been an ever changing scene. The size of companies, their products and methods of manufacture, and the number of employees have varied enormously. Some firms ceased trading soon after arriving in the town, others expanded and became stable businesses, even in what were some difficult times. Others amalgamated and merged with other companies and changed ownership. By the end of the 20th century, of the many companies that arrived in Thetford as 'Overspill' firms, many had not survived. [Photograph courtesy of Thetford Town Council]

THERMOS, c.1963 & 1965

Thermos Ltd the world famous makers of vacuum flasks since 1907, began production at Tottenham in 1908 before moving to Brentwood, Essex. The Thetford factory, built on a 13 acre [5 hectare] site for the manufacture of glass vacuum bottles for flasks, began production in 1965. They were the first to do so on the Caxton Way Industrial Estate. The head office remained at Brentwood, Essex.

It was only after the commitment of large companies such as Thermos, health product manufacturer Baxter Laboratories and Danish bacon processor and supplier Danepak to move their factories to Thetford, that London County Council and Thetford Borough Council could, with more certainty, feel confident that Thetford's 'Overspill' scheme be deemed a successful venture. The Thermos factory, with its large and distinctive roof cowls or vents, was a familiar outline on the Thetford industrial landscape for four decades.

In 1974 the Thermos plant was employing 270 people and there was more optimism after a large extension to the factory was built for a new plastic moulding and assembly line in 1996. By then the company was Japanese owned and in 1999, it was announced that production at Thetford was to cease. By November the following year, 330 workers had been made redundant and all production at Thetford had ceased. Production was moved to China. [Photographs courtesy of Thetford Town Council]

REDCASTLE FURZE ESTATE, c.1972

In 1963, plans were published for a new housing estate to be built on land between the London Road and Brandon Road. Work began in about 1964 and by 1970, 700 new homes had been completed, creating St Martin's Way, Canons Walk and St John's Way to form the Redcastle Furze Estate. Moreover, a parade of six shops opened in 1967 and the Redcastle Furze Primary School opened in January the following year.

The London Road can be seen running diagonally in the top right corner of the photograph. St Martin's Way stands alongside. Canons Walk runs parallel to the London Road, dividing St Martins Way and St John's Way, the central segment in the photograph. In the bottom left corner is McKenzie Road, a private development and the Caxton Way Industrial Estate can be seen in the bottom right corner. [Photograph courtesy of Thetford Town Council]

ST JOHN'S WAY, REDCASTLE FURZE ESTATE, c.1967

The principle plan for the Redcastle Furze Estate was the segregation of pedestrians and motor vehicles. Some houses were built around small courtyards, while running through the centre of the estate is the Canons Walk, making it possible to walk to the town centre without having to cross a road. The estate is also connected to the north side of the Little Ouse River and the Abbey Estate by a pedestrian underpass at the Brandon Road and Blaydon Bridge over the river. A loop road, St John's Way, runs around the edge of the estate. [Photographs courtesy of John Ayton]

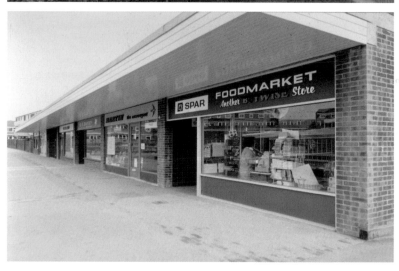

ABBEY FARM ESTATE, c.1971

Agricultural work on the ancient Abbey Farm ceased in 1962 and early the following year the farm equipment was sold by public auction. The redundant farm buildings, an assortment of barns and cottages standing adjacent to the ruins of the medieval Cluniac Priory, survived to the end of the century although their future was uncertain. In 1965, two years after the auction, plans were released for building one thousand homes on agricultural land that once formed part of the Abbey Farm. The new residential development was to be called the Abbey Farm Estate.

In 1967, about the same time as construction work began on the new housing estate, a new road was constructed off the Station Road to form a junction with the Brandon Road. This road was to be the main road through the new estate and was later named Canterbury Way.

The first houses to be completed on the Abbey Farm estate were handed over to Thetford Borough Council at a special ceremony in June 1968. In May 1970 it was reported that large numbers of Jeyes' employees were moving on to the Abbey Farm Estate. One of the first new shops to open on the Abbey Farm Estate was the 'Buy Wise' Spar store in May 1971. [Photographs courtesy of Studio Five, Thetford]

BRUNEL WAY INDUSTRIAL ESTATE, c.1975

Work began clearing land north of the town, between the Mundford Road and the railway, for the construction of Thetford's third industrial estate, Brunel Way, in September 1966. In 1968 work began on the construction of the largest factory by far on the Brunel Way Industrial Estate. This was a reported £2m factory and office block on a 17½ acre [7 hectare] site, for Jeyes Group Ltd of Barking and Plaistow, Essex. The Jeyes factory and office block can be seen just right of centre in the photograph, adjacent to the railway. While the new factory was being constructed, 900 people from Jeyes' headquarters made a total of eighteen coach trips to Thetford, to view the new factory and the town. Perhaps they were fortunate to get a glimpse of the town before deciding whether to make the move to Thetford. Some families arrived from London with their firms, never having visited the town.

Jeyes new factory went into production in April 1970, initially producing toilet rolls. Soon afterwards, work began in the bulk filling department from where disinfectants and washing up liquids from their well-known brand of household cleaning products are dispatched.

In 1983 Breckland District Council published a *'Directory of Manufacturing and Processing Firms in Breckland District'*, and listed one hundred and thirty firms on Thetford's industrial estates; seventeen were located on Brunel Way. By 1996, a Breckland *'Industrial Directory',* listed 198 firms including warehouses, retail outlets and others on the industrial estates.

From the early 1970s, work began on the opposite side of the Mundford Road creating the Fison Way Industrial Estate. During the 1960s and 70s, with so much construction work planned and in progress, it was a 'boom' time for builders in Thetford. However, once the demand for building work began to slacken in the 1980s, some construction workers found employment in factories on the industrial estates they had helped to build.

The small, separate industrial estate that was named Telford Way can be seen on the left of the Jeyes site. In 1983 eight companies were operating from there. The factory in the left foreground is Nichol Beauty Products Ltd. [Photograph courtesy of Thetford Town Council]

NORFOLK COUNTY LIBRARY, from TANNER STREET, c.1969 & WELL STREET c.1970

Besides the new housing and industrial estates that were planned directly as 'overspill' developments, numerous other projects involved the construction of all sorts of buildings to provide additional or increased services and needs for Thetford's rapidly increasing population, mostly new families with children of school age arriving in the town. Educational facilities were a priority and besides several new schools built on or close to the new housing estates in the 1960s and 70s, a new library was built and opened in 1970.

THE COURT HOUSE, c.1980

Another new building to appear in the 1970s was the Magistrates' Court House for taking the preliminary hearings of the more serious criminal offences and dealing with petty offences, matrimonial cases, licensing duties and many other subjects besides. A malt house and other buildings once associated with Thetford's once important maltings industry were demolished in the early 1970s to make way for the new Magistrates' Court that was opened by the Lord Chief Justice, Lord Wiggery, in September 1974. The Magistrates' Court had previously been held in the Guildhall, as were other courts of law for several centuries past. In the foreground is the river Thet and Butten Island.

NUNSGATE, 1965

Soon after the arrival of the first firms from London, the local private housing market was unable to meet the demand from the influx of business owners and their senior staff, who had moved to Thetford. Initially, many had no choice but to rent temporarily local authority or private accommodation until suitable housing became available. Work on the Redgate Estate began in 1960 and was the first large, private housing development since the 'overspill' had been agreed in the mid-1950s. It was soon followed by Abbeygate in 1962 and Nunsgate 1964. In 1965, Nunsgate was known as the 'Nuns Bridges' development, when local estate agents Hawker & Witton offered houses there for sale from £4,430. [Photograph courtesy of Thetford Town Council]

ELIZABETH WATLING CLOSE, 1976

Work began constructing the last residential development under the town expansion agreement, the so-called 'Ladies Estate', in March 1974. Each road on the estate was named after prominent or well known women. Elizabeth Watling was Mayor of Thetford 1950-51 and another lady commemorated on the estate is Sybil Wheeler who was Mayor for two consecutive years in the mid-1950s. The estate originally comprised 357 three-bedroom houses, 34 four-bedroom houses, 57 one-bedroom bungalows, 59 two-bedroom bungalows and 52 one-bedroom flats and was completed in 1979. In the period between 1958 and 1978, a total of 3,500 local authority houses had been built. It was a considerable achievement. [Photograph courtesy of Studio Five, Thetford]

KEEPING THETFORD TIDY

'Thetford's mayor on Tuesday threatened to lead a campaign to get the town out of Breckland District if street cleaning was not improved.' Thetford & Watton Times, 22 February 1980

BOROUGH of THETFORD, REFUSE CARTS, 1938

Before 1892, when the Borough of Thetford first adopted a regular household refuse collection, the town's inhabitants had few choices for the disposal of the small amounts of rubbish they accumulated. It was either burnt or buried in gardens and yards, dumped at one of the rubbish pits located around the periphery of the town or wherever convenient.

The Corporation refuse cart was horse-drawn until 1938, when it was replaced by the small motor lorry seen in this photograph. The town's night-soil or 'honey' cart, however, continued to be horse-drawn, at least, until sometime during the 1939-45 War. The night soil was tipped into pits just off the Bury Road, close to where Queensway is today. The Corporation rubbish dump on the Melford Common was officially abandoned in 1937, when a former gravel pit on the Mundford Road was utilised for the town's rubbish. Another rubbish dump was later established on the Croxton Road.

THE ABBEY FARM DEPOT, 1975

Thetford Borough Council had its 'works' depot for many years in outbuildings close to the Guildhall, then in the mid 1960s the Abbey Farm was acquired and became a council works depot for the expanding 'works' department, including the refuse and waste disposal services. In 1970, Thetford Borough Council's dustmen, road sweepers, gardeners and sewage workers were amongst those involved in industrial action when they implemented an overtime ban in a dispute for a pay increase.

In 1974, Breckland District Council became the new authority for many services and responsibilities previously under the jurisdiction of Thetford Borough Council, including the weekly collection of household waste. The Abbey Farm depot finally closed in the early 1990s and remained redundant for the remainder of the century, its future uncertain.

KING STREET, 1987

One of Thetford's best remembered road sweepers is Fred 'Colonel Moke' Lockwood [1902-1973], who worked for the Borough Council for 30 years, both as a road sweeper and dustman. In Fred's day people would often stop and pass the time of day with the council's road sweepers. There is one amusing story of a lady in Croxton Road, who telephoned the Town Clerk to ask if he could immediately remove the gentleman road sweeper from outside the front of her house. Apparently, he had been leaning on his broom for such a long time she had become alarmed that the broom handle might pass clean through his body.

MECHANICAL ROAD SWEEPER, BUTTEN BRIDGE, 1986

In 1966 Thetford Borough Council sought to buy a mechanical road sweeper, to complement the small team of men equipped with brooms, shovels and handcarts that endeavoured to keep the town's roads and pavements clean and free of litter. That same year, Thetford Borough Council also purchased a second refuse cart to cope with the increasing number of households. By then the town's population had reached 10,000.

SCRAPYARD, ST NICHOLAS STREET, 1988

Over the decades, both local and itinerant rag-and-bone dealers, scrap merchants and others have scoured Thetford's streets, collecting an assortment of materials from households, such as glass bottles and jars, newspaper, cardboard, rags, rabbit skins, scrap metal and any other item deemed to have some economic value. During the 1939-45 War the collection of metal, not only scrap but also useful household articles, fixtures and fittings, was an important government scheme for providing material for the manufacture of military equipment such as aircraft and armaments.

This scrap yard in St Nicholas Street was established about 1930, soon after the closure of the St Nicholas Works and by the time that this photograph was taken, it was specializing in second-hand parts for motor vehicles.

THE THETFORD SOCIETY, 1990

In the 1980s and early 1990s, Thetford's litter problem was probably at its worst, for all sorts of reasons. Local organisations such as The Thetford Society, Chamber of Commerce and Women's Institute organised regular litter 'pick-ups' in an effort to 'Keep Thetford Tidy'. In this photograph, on a bright, sunny morning in February, 1990, members of the Thetford Society, armed with black bin liners and protective gloves, are joined at the Castle Park by a few ladies from Thetford WI. At least six large bags of rubbish and other items were collected by the volunteers in two hours. In 1991 a National Spring Clean Week was held following a new Environment Protection Act.

HOUSEHOLD REFUSE SITE, BURRELL WAY, 1986

A Thetford Environment Action Group was formed in 1972 and by 1974 a recycling centre for glass, rags and paper was opened in the Tanner Street car park, on the site of the old tannery. Other recycling centres were soon established in other parts of the town. Certainly from the 1970s, as local land-fill sites became full and new, potential sites more difficult to find, the disposal and recycling of all kinds of general, household and industrial waste and materials became a major issue for local authorities, private enterprises and the general public.

This household waste site was opened on the former Airscrew Weyroc site in 1984, replacing several portable rubbish skips that had been located about the town.

PEARSONS, TELFORD WAY, 1981

Before the end of the 20th century, Pearsons waste disposal and recycling service had developed into a large business, providing a valuable service to the town and surrounding district. It began at Brandon in 1945 with Cyril Pearson collecting waste paper and cardboard from local households. Six years later, Cyril started trading from a few old sheds off Thetford's Brandon Road and, as the business grew, moved to Lime Kiln Lane in 1966. In the 1970s, Pearsons continued to expand and moved to Telford Way in 1974. By the time that another new and much larger depot was opened at Fison Way in 1995, the company was in the hands of Cyril's son, Pat and grandson, Jo. By then they were operating a fleet of 24 vehicles and hundreds of portable skips for the collection and disposal of all sorts of waste, including hazardous materials.

This photograph captures three generations. From left-right: Jo, Pat and Cyril Pearson. [Photograph courtesy of Pearsons]

FIRE! FIRE! FIRE!

'A Coroner has praised brave neighbours and firemen for their frantic efforts to try to save a family from their burning home.' Inquest following a fire at St John's Way, Thetford.
Bury Free Press, 11 April 1986

BOROUGH OF THETFORD FIRE BRIGADE, 1905

At the very beginning of the 20th century, the Borough Fire Brigade attended local fires with a manual, horse-drawn fire engine purchased new in the 1870s, just a few years before the brigade was formed in 1880. After a brand-new Merryweather steam fire engine was purchased in 1905, the Borough Fire Brigade was reorganised and was then considered to be a modern fire service. This photograph was taken outside the Cage Lane Fire Station, soon after the delivery of the new steam fire engine.

THE GRAMMAR SCHOOL PLAINS, 1905

Thetford's firemen pose proudly with the new Merryweather steam fire engine on the Grammar School Plains, beside the Brandon Road. The steam fire engine was purchased by the Corporation in February 1905 at a cost of £325 [including £65 that was raised by public subscription]. The 'steamer' was horse-drawn until 1921, when a special tow bar was fitted so that it could be hauled by a motor vehicle. This system continued until 1930, when the Thetford Fire Brigade was loaned a former motor 'luggage bus' that had been used by Lord Iveagh at nearby Elveden Hall. The former 'luggage bus' was soon converted into a fire tender and modified to pull the steam fire engine. Thetford could then boast that they were a fully motorised brigade. It was 1938 before the 'steamer' was replaced by a brand-new, motor fire engine, a Dennis 'Ace'.

THE PULP WORKS, MILL LANE, c.1945

The year before war was declared in September 1939, auxiliary firemen were recruited to give support and assistance, if needed, to the Borough of Thetford Fire Brigade. Once war was declared, one of Thetford's Auxiliary Fire Service [AFS] units was based at the 'pulp works' of Thetford Moulded Products.

By May 1941, many large cities and other parts of the country had suffered infernos and damage as a result of enemy bombing and in September that year, the nation's fire brigades were nationalized in an effort to meet the demands that such an extreme situation presented.

THETFORD UNIT, NATIONAL FIRE SERVICE [NFS], CAGE LANE, 1947

As Thetford was surrounded by numerous airfields, training areas and other operational military sites during the war, it was a very busy period for the Thetford Fire Brigade. They were often reinforced by fire brigades from places much further afield because of the high number of major incidents in the surrounding countryside. Several of the firemen in this photograph served as retained or auxiliary firemen during the war.

MILL LANE, 1956

Certainly from the 1920s, this area beside the Little Ouse river was frequently used by Thetford's firemen as a training ground, to practise drills and test the appliances and equipment. This photograph captures Thetford's retained or part-time firemen with a new, aluminium bodied, 'Commer' fire engine or appliance that had just been delivered. It replaced the Dennis 'Ace' fire engine that had been in service since 1938. Standing in the background is an ex-War Department vehicle that had been painted red and specially adapted for fighting heath and forest fires.

THETFORD RETAINED FIREMEN, 1987

Ever since the Borough of Thetford Fire Brigade was formed in 1880, there has never been a shortage of local men coming forward to serve as volunteer or retained firemen. In the early years of the century, firemen were summoned to a fire by the sound of an exploding maroon. Later electric sirens and call-bells in the firemen's homes were used before electronic pocket 'alerters' were introduced in 1972.

Tuesday evening has traditionally been drill night for the town's volunteer firemen, when they test the appliances and equipment and practise dealing with many situations.

STATION ROAD, 1946

During the century, Thetford's firemen have been called to numerous fires in the town, from chimney fires of no real consequence to large blazes that have resulted in the destruction of valuable property and even a few that have tragically claimed lives. Firemen can be seen dousing the remains of the Station Road showrooms and workshops of local builder Goddards.

THERMOS, CAXTON WAY, 1965

The local commons, heaths and forests, particularly during the dry summer months, have been a frequent source of fire. Another is industrial premises. Thermos had only been trading from Thetford a few months when fire broke out in the early hours of the morning and destroyed this large warehouse, despite the efforts of 9 water tenders and their crews.

RAYMOND STREET, 1980

Large conflagrations or fires often draw a crowd of spectators to view the spectacle and the efforts of the fire brigade. These maltings, like many others in the town, were badly damaged by fire. Fortunately these once important industrial buildings, that formed part of a 19th century brewery, were later refurbished.

GRAMMAR SCHOOL, LONDON ROAD, 1980

Over the centuries, acts of arson have probably been the cause of many fires that have damaged or totally destroyed numerous local buildings. One of those lost forever is the thatched Grammar School sports pavilion that stood on the playing fields beside the London Road.

MINSTERGATE, 1986

The local fire service at the end of the century compared very favourably with that maintained in the town, at least, in the first six decades of the century, similarly with equipment, resources, skills and training. Even so, Fogarty's feather cleaning plant is yet another industrial building to suffer from the ravages of fire.

THE MARKET PLACE, 1990

During the century, much has continued to be done to prevent fires and to protect lives and property. Building regulations have improved as has the use and storage of flammable materials. Moreover, the provision of fire extinguishers, fire escapes, fire alarms, smoke detectors and much more besides, has helped to make Thetford a safer place in which to live and work.

THETFORD FIRE STATION, NORWICH ROAD, 1988

From the 1st July 1948, following the Fire Service Act 1947, Norfolk County Council became the local fire authority. All over the country, fire services were gradually modernised, creating an improved, efficient service through the standardisation of equipment, training and many other elements. At Thetford, local builders Goddards, began constructing a new fire station on the Norwich Road in 1952. The following year the appliances were moved into the newly completed two-bay fire station.

Since opening, the fire station has been modernised and enlarged on several occasions. The first of these was in 1956 when a recreation and briefing room, pantry and store were added. At that time, Thetford's firemen were alerted and summoned to the fire station by a siren, fixed high up between two large wooden posts, standing beside the station.

THETFORD FIRE STATION, NORWICH ROAD, 1988

As the town's population rapidly increased, there was certainly a greater demand on Thetford's part-time retained firemen. Their burden was lessened to some extent after full-time firemen were stationed at Thetford from 1975. By then the fire service had become a multi-faceted emergency and rescue service, equipped and trained to deal with a wide-range of incidents such as chemical spills, explosions, fires, floods, rail and air crashes, to name but a few. Perhaps the most frequent incident during the last three decades of the century was the road traffic accident.

PEOPLE DRESSED UP

'We never went to a fire dressed in our uniforms, they had to be kept "spick and span" for parades, we just went in whatever clothes we were wearing, plus our brass helmets, boots and firemen's belt.'
Former Thetford fireman, Tom Vincent talking about the 1930s.
David Osborne, *'A History of the Borough of Thetford Fire Brigade',* published 1988

THE MAYOR, RICHARD P.F. EASTEN, 1964

Fifty-eight different people served as the Mayor of Thetford during the 20th century. Dr Alain Glaisyer Minns [1858-1930], was Mayor of the Borough of Thetford in 1904 and had the distinction of being Britain's first black mayor. Lucy Emma Bidwell was the first woman to be Mayor of the Borough of Thetford in 1928. During the century, she was followed by twelve other women, some of whom served as Mayor more than once. Leslie Broadhurst who was Mayor in 1972, was the first to have come to the town with the 'overspill'. Jack Ramm who was the last Mayor of the Borough of Thetford, also has the distinction of being the first Mayor of Thetford Town Council in 1974. Only one other, Terence J. Lamb, served as Mayor for both Thetford Borough Council and Thetford Town Council. [Photograph courtesy of Studio Five, Thetford]

THE MARKET PLACE, 1951

Throughout the century, many Thetfordians have continued to dress in special garments or uniforms, displaying an office, rank or representing some local organisation, such as a military unit, local school or sports team for example. A civic procession is just one occasion when several uniformed organisations appear together in the town. In this photograph, Thetford's Anglican choirs lead the procession, followed by many other local organisations during Thetford's 'Festival of Britain'. In a special booklet published to commemorate this event, A.D.J. Brooks wrote, *"In 1951 Festival Year, Thetford is a town of 4,500 people, set in Breckland at the meeting of the Little Ouse and Thet. A town the scene of an historic past, still capable of meeting the challenge of the future."*

ST PETER'S CHURCH CHOIR, c.1950

Members of St Peter's Choir pose outside the west door of the church for this photograph, specially commissioned to show off their new robes. Front row, left-right: Billy Filby, Richard O'Nians, Mary Ellis, Cynthia Hensby, Pauline Hubbard, Judy Hensby, Pat Pearson, Edward Rosier. Second row: Douglas Whalebelly, Vera Berry, Daisy Holmes (organist), Mrs Rosier. Third row: Mrs Warner, Rev. Reginald Jackson, Dorothy Watson. Back row: Margaret Warner, Mrs Lake. [Photograph courtesy of Cynthia Royle]

THETFORD STATION, 1938

The Automobile Association first introduced scout patrols, albeit on bicycles, in 1907 two years after the formation of the AA. It was probably after the 1914-18 War before uniformed AA scouts were seen in Thetford. A contentious advertisement at Thetford's railway station announcing, "It's Quicker By Rail", provides a backdrop to the AA Scouts, gathered from all over Norfolk and Suffolk, not only showing off their smart uniforms but parading their newly delivered fleet of forty-nine BSA motorcycles. The gentleman standing is AA Superintendent, Mr P. Yarnall.

ODDFELLOWS HALL, 1948

Besides the formal occasions when people have dressed up, there have been numerous opportunities for Thetfordians to 'let their hair down' and dress in clothing that, in public, they would not normally wear. This photograph captures Miss Pat Boughen, dressed as Robb Wilton's fireman, and the winner of a fancy dress competition held at a dance in the Oddfellows Hall. "The day war broke out", is a famous phrase from one of Robb Wilton's very popular radio comedy shows in the 1930s and 40s and one of his best known radio characters was a fireman, doggedly trying to remember the route to a house on fire! The gentleman holding the ladder is the master of ceremonies Mr Sefton. [Photograph courtesy of Pat Boughen]

THE RECREATION GROUND, c.1960

Fancy dress competitions and parties, have long been popular for young and old. These young ladies, employees of local company Cathodeon Ltd., are taking part in a fancy dress competition dressed as pupils of the popular, fictional boarding school, St Trinian's. Left-right: 'Dotty' Woods, Pat Debenham, Barbara Hemstock, Anne ?, Geraldine Chamberlain, Geraldine Cooke, Janet Johnson, Patsy Scott. [Photograph courtesy of Neville Lockwood]

OLD MARKET STREET, 1980

Some are wearing fancy dress at the start of a pancake relay race from outside the Dolphin public house. The races were organised by the landlord of the Dolphin public house, not only to provide some fun for the competitors and spectators but also to raise funds for a local charity. The winning men's team was Phil Wright, Mick McDonald, Gordon Scott and Phil Redman. The winning ladies team, Ruth Benbow, Moira McCandlesses, Wendy Raphael and Mary Williams. [Photograph courtesy of Archant]

THETFORD ST JOHN AMBULANCE BRIGADE, KING STREET, c.1980

Uniformed members of the St John Ambulance Brigade have been seen about the town since a brigade was formed at Thetford in 1937. These members of the Thetford St John Brigade are wearing the universal T-shirt emblazoned with the St John badge or emblem. Amongst those taking part in this sponsored bed push to raise funds for the St John Brigade are Clare and Mrs Brewster, Eileen & Trevor Roberts, James, Jane and Mrs Phyllis Warren, Hayley Bishop, Lorraine Parslow and Mark Raynor.

RIVERSIDE CAR PARK, 1992

Is this someone in fancy dress? No, it's Postman Pat who was visiting Thetford in his special post van as part of the Thetford Carnival. Postman Pat was popularized by a children's animated television programme first screened in 1981 and was later adopted by the Royal Mail to promote postal services.

Are those young boys asking, "Where's Mrs Goggins?" or "Where's Jess?"

THE MARKET PLACE, c.1955

Uniformed postmen were about the town in the very early years of the 20th century, when there were just three Thetford postmen and certainly no motor post vans. However, as the postal services and the number of postal staff increased during the century, a new Post Office was opened in 1939, adjacent to the Post Office that had opened in the 1890s. By the time that this photograph was taken in front of the Post Office, there were at least twenty-one postmen and a fleet of twelve motor vans. Moreover, for a few weeks each year in the Christmas period, additional sorting office facilities and about 50 temporary postal staff were introduced to cope with the increased volume of mail.

THETFORD GIRLS' BRIGADE, c.1972

There were numerous uniformed organisations for young people in the town during the 20th century. One of the first was a Boys' Brigade in the very early years of the 20th century and then a troop of Boy Scouts from 1910. Girl Guides were first formed in the town in 1917 but it was 1971 before a Girls' Brigade was formed with their distinctive uniforms and headdress. When first formed, the Girls' Brigade held its meetings at the Fulmerston Road Baptist Church. [Photograph courtesy of Kathy Rae]

WHITE HART STREET, 2000

The 20th century was really over when the second part of *Thetford A Century Remembered* was launched at the Ancient House Museum. There were a countless number of different events held in the town during the century, occasions when Thetfordians shared some time together, if only for a few hours. We have shared so many human emotions. Together we have applauded, celebrated, commemorated, laughed, commiserated, mourned, prayed and stood in silence.

Most of us, in varying degrees, will have been a part of 20th century Thetford, a period that has probably been the most tumultuous in the town's long history. It certainly ought to be a century worth remembering. [Photograph courtesy of Studio Five, Thetford]

THETFORD'S MAYORS 1900-2000

'It shall be lawful for the mayor and all succeeding mayors, whilst they execute the office of mayor in the same borough, to have a man carrying or bearing a sword before them, for the time being.'
Thetford Charter of Incorporation granted by Queen Elizabeth in 1574

Borough of Thetford

Year	Mayor
1899-1900	Stephen Oldman, jnr
1900-01	Walter C. Fison
1901-02	Walter C. Fison
1902-03	Charles Burrell, jnr
1903-04	Charles Burrell, jnr
1904-05	Allan G. Minns
1905-06	Allan G. Minns
1906-07	Frederick H. Millington
1907-08	Frederick H. Millington
1908-09	Robert Tilley
1909-10	Robert Tilley
1910-11	Robert Tilley
1911-12	George Brown
1912-13	George Brown
1913-14	Robert Tilley, Charles Burrell
1914-15	Charles Burrell
1915-16	Stephen Oldman
1916-17	Stephen Oldman
1917-18	Stephen Oldman
1918-19	Stephen Oldman
1919-20	John G. Brown
1920-21	John G. Brown
1921-22	John G. Brown
1922-23	William Lambert
1923-24	William Lambert
1924-25	John E. Meek
1925-26	John E. Meek
1926-27	Stephen Oldman, Thomas R. Doran
1927-28	Thomas R. Doran
1928-29	Lucy E. Bidwell
1929-30	Lucy E. Bidwell
1930-31	Isaac B. Aspland
1931-32	Isaac B. Aspland
1932-33	John G. Brown, Sir William Gentle KB
1933-34	Sir William Gentle KB
1934-35	Sir William Gentle KB
1935-36	George Squires
1936-37	Sir William Gentle KB
1937-38	Stanley G. Brown
1938-39	George E. Lambert
1939-40	George E. Lambert
1940-41	Sir William Gentle KB
1941-42	Henry W. Watling
1942-43	Henry W. Watling
1943-44	Arthur S. Law
1944-45	Arthur S. Law
1945-46	Cyril J. Sear
1946-47	Stanley G. Brown
1947-48	Horatio J. Leech
1948-49	Horatio J. Leech
1949-50	Benjamin C. Culey
1950-51	Elizabeth Watling
1951-52	George R. Blaydon
1952-53	Sybil M. Wheeler
1953-54	George E. Lambert
1954-55	Sybil M. Wheeler
1955-56	Sybil M. Wheeler
1956-57	George A. Kybird
1957-58	Harry W. Johnson
1958-59	Harry W. Johnson
1959-60	Marjorie I. Sutherland
1960-61	Marjorie I. Sutherland
1961-62	Doris Anderson
1962-63	John, Lord Fisher of Kilverstone
1963-64	John, Lord Fisher of Kilverstone
1964-65	Richard P.F. Easten
1965-66	Richard P.F. Easten
1966-67	James T. Waters
1967-68	James T. Waters
1968-69	Benjamin C. Culey
1969-70	Benjamin C. Culey
1970-71	Terence J. Lamb
1971-72	John T. Mayes
1972-73	Leslie Broadhurst
1973-74	Jack E. Ramm

Thetford Town Council

Year	Mayor
1974-75	Jack E. Ramm
1975-76	Henry R. Crampton
1976-77	John W.F. Sweeney
1977-78	Walter Nunn
1978-79	Frederick R.J. Room
1979-80	Colin W. Armes
1980-81	Mary E. Page
1981-82	Doris C. Perkins
1982-83	Francis M. Kew
1983-84	Gary McGinty
1984-85	Lieselotte Frost
1985-86	Michael E. Edmund
1986-87	Frederick H. Attfield
1987-88	Freda M. Wilkes
1988-89	Kathleen E. Key
1989-90	Terence J. Lamb
1990-91	Thelma I. Paines
1991-92	Gary McGinty
1992-93	Pamela M. Van Weegen
1993-94	Kathleen E. Key
1994-95	Colin W. Armes
1995-96	Paul W. Brooker
1996-97	Patrick J. Pearson
1997-98	Raymond S. Key
1998-99	Derek Serjeant
1999-2000	Jennifer Bullock

1900 Severe influenza in the town causes 100 men to be absent from the Burrell Works. Concert in Oddfellows Hall raised £22 16s 2d for the Transvaal War. A total of 13 houses erected in Vicarage Road. Attempted rape of a girl on Barnham Cross Common. **1901** Death of Queen Victoria. Income from the Thetford Navigation for the year "absolutely nothing". Very strong gales played havoc with the flags flying from the towers of the local churches, tearing them to pieces and beyond further use. A workman killed after falling from scaffolding during the construction of the new Guildhall. New Conservative Club opened in White Hart Street. **1902** Coronation of King Edward VII. Opening of new Guildhall. Householders warned not tot leave their homes unsecured after dusk during the Coronation celebrations. HM Don Carlos, King of Portugal, inspects the local militia at the railway station en-route to Elveden Hall. **1903** Thetford Town FC to form a second XI. A wagon on the Market Place promoting emigration to Canada. Council School Inspector's report makes mention of smoking amongst the boys. **1904** Tramps charged with sleeping in the open-air on the Bury Road and Castle Meadow, discharged after promising to leave the town at once. Yeomanry Ball held for the Thetford Troop of the Yorks Own Loyal Suffolk Hussars. Death of G.E. Bond, gunsmith, aged 65 years. **1905** Local debate on the subject of whether the town's telegraph and telephone cables should be concealed below the ground or suspended from posts above. Gramophone selection presented to railway workers, at their dinner held at Dog & Partridge pub. Complaints about the poor state of Thetford's roads, "now little else than puddle". **1906** Town Council proposes to water the roads on a Sunday to keep the dust down. John Lee, a tramp, sent to prison for 14 days with hard labour, for begging in Magdalen Street. First agm of YMCA. Balance sheet for Thetford's soup kitchens published. **1907** Wesleyan Sunday School celebrates its centenary. Dedication of new rood-screen at St Mary's Church. Auction of poultry, sheep, horses and carts at the Thetford sale yard, Station Road. **1908** Borough Council undertakes the complete scavanging of the town, including the emptying of all privy vaults and cesspools. Board of Guardians report 141 inmates resident at the workhouse. Calls for a clamp-down on illicit gambling at cards in the town. **1909** First annual dinner held for Old Boys' of Thetford Grammar School. A woman pleaded guilty to using indecent language in Bury Road and was fined 10/-. Temporary theatre erected near the Bridge Tavern. **1910** Death of King Edward VII. King George V Proclamation ceremony and parade on the Market Place. Coroner's Inquest on William Dodd, killed while using a drill at the Burrell Works. Thetford Boy Scouts inspected by General Baden-Powell. **1911** Coronation of King George V. Retirement of Mr Levick, Thetford postman for 43 years. Boxing tournament at the Oddfellows Hall. Gypsies moved off Barnham Cross Common by the common holders. **1912** Royal Norfolk Show held at Thetford. Thetford Union Board of Guardians to provide spectacles for poor children. Formation of Thetford Women's Suffragette Society. **1913** Motor cyclists attempt to conquer Castle Hill. Cinema opens in Guildhall Street. Carnival held on the river. **1914** War declared. Closure of the White Hart Inn. Oddfellows Hall granted a cinema licence. **1915** National Registration Act –

Thetford divided into 21 districts and all aged between 15 and 65 years on 15 August to register. Death of local businessman, W. Boughton, aged 75 years. **1916** War restrictions, closure of Thetford's pubs at 9pm. Fear of Zeppelin raids, residents fined for not shading lights. Thetford Small-Pox Hospital destroyed by fire. **1917** King's Proclamation for the necessity of saving food, was read by the Mayor. Public meeting in the Guildhall, 'Economy in War Time'. Several public houses closed during Whitsuntide owing to a lack of beer. Thetford mother given 6 months hard labour for neglecting her children. **1918** Notice given that blasts from the steam siren at the electricity station to give warning of air raids. Sgt Major Horwood, Essex Regt and clerk at the Burrell Works, awarded DCM. Thetford War Agricultural Committee report that 1,654 acres of land in district ploughed by tractors. Peace declared. **1919** Thetford Union's Board of Guardians report an increase in vagrancy. Fatal accident at the Bell corner. Old Elizabethan house in White Hart Street sold at auction for £500. **1920** Charles Burrell & Sons' St Nicholas Works taken over by Agricultural & General Engineers Ltd. Closure and sale of horses and carriages from Mrs Pye's posting establishment, Castle Street. **1921** Public baths installed in the Town Hall. Reported that between 50-90 horses are grazing on the Barnham Cross Common. The Ancient House handed over to the Corporation. **1922** Thetford's ex-servicemen propose to erect a club hut. Great War memorial unveiled at the Boys' Grammar School. 85 inmates at Thetford Union Workhouse and 35 vagrants relieved 1-14th June. **1923** A hydro-electric scheme proposed to supply electricity to Brandon & Thetford by harnessing the Little Ouse river. Death of Mr Arthur J. Savage, senior partner of Savage Bros., King Street. **1924** Royal Norfolk Show held at Thetford. At a Borough Council meeting it was asked if something could be done with regard to a speed limit for motorists in the town. **1925** Death of Charlie Thrower, who started work at the age of 10 years and was employed at the Burrell Works for 60 years. **1926** A stand for spectators is erected at the 'Rec'. Death of the Mayor, J.E. Meek. **1927** Exhibition of paintings bequeathed to the town by Price Frederick Duleep Singh. Closure of the Globe, Kings Arms, and White Horse public houses. **1928** Burrells deny rumours the St Nicholas Works is to close. German Gun a souvenir of the Great War is removed from the Castle Park. Number 33 Earls Street, the former Globe pub, is sold for £310. **1929** Death of Charles Burrell jnr. Thetford Debating Society debate the question, 'Is Democracy A Failure?'. Thetford's clergy report a decline in numbers attending church. Death of Abraham Cash, landlord of the Green Dragon for over 50 years. Rate payers complain to the Town Council about traction engines emitting excessive smoke when passing through the town. **1930** At a meeting of Thetford Town Council it was decided to purchase instruments for measuring the rainfall in the borough. A Cycling Club formed. Thetford Board of Guardians decide to give inmates of the workhouse butter in lieu of margarine. **1931** Boxing tournament held at the Oddfellows Hall in aid of the Cottage Hospital. Thetford Debating Society discuss 'The Influence of the Cinema.' Thetford's County Library to reopen to children on Tuesdays and adults on Thursdays. **1932** First staunch blown-up by Royal Engineers. Opening of extension to the Girls' Grammar